Leadership Evolution: Navigating the Tapestry
of Faith and Politics for Sustainable Governance

POWER
TRANSFORMATION

A Timely Necessity

AINAN AHMAD

BLUEROSE PUBLISHERS
India | U.K.

Copyright © Ainan Ahmad 2024

All rights reserved by author. No part of this publication may be reproduced, stored in a retrieval system or transmitted in any form or by any means, electronic, mechanical, photocopying, recording or otherwise, without the prior permission of the author. Although every precaution has been taken to verify the accuracy of the information contained herein, the publisher assumes no responsibility for any errors or omissions. No liability is assumed for damages that may result from the use of information contained within.

BlueRose Publishers takes no responsibility for any damages, losses, or liabilities that may arise from the use or misuse of the information, products, or services provided in this publication.

For permissions requests or inquiries regarding this publication, please contact:

BLUEROSE PUBLISHERS
www.BlueRoseONE.com
info@bluerosepublishers.com
+91 8882 898 898
+4407342408967

ISBN: 978-93-5989-050-0

Cover Design: Muskan Sachdeva
Typesetting: Pooja Sharma

First Edition: January 2024

Contents

Chapter One: Introduction 1

1.1 Background and Justification 1

1.2 Area and Restrictions 4

1.3 Methods: Design of Research 5

1.4 Setting Up the Research 7

Chapter Two: Romanand Parsian History and the Transfer of Power in Human History 9

2.1 Early Concepts of Governance and Power 9

2.2 Roman Republic: A Power Transfer Case Study 11

2.3 The Roman Republic's Decline 12

2.4 Roman Empire and Its Successors 13

2.5 Experienced a Crisis Characterised by Frequent Military Takeovers, Usurpations, and Assassinations. 14

2.6 A Case Study of the Roman Kingdom on the Development of Power Transfer 16

2.7 Roman Monarchy: An Historical Overview 17

2.8 The Roman Republic's Mechanisms for Power Transfer 20

2.9 Power Transfer Evolution: Insights from the Roman Republic 23

2.10 A Historical View of the Development of Power Transfer Using the Roman Empire 29

2.11 Political Institutions in the Republic Of Rome . 35

2.12 The Parthian Empire's Formation and the Power-Transition Crisis of the 160s-130s BCE 72

2.13 IR Theory and Parthia's Ascent 75

2.14 The Breakdown Occurs 81

2.15 The Median Conquest by the Parthians 96

2.16 The Challenging Western Frontier of the Parthians 103

Chapter Three: Power Transition; a Case Study of Vladimir Putin and Xi Jinping 115

3.1 Christian Principles and Values 115

3.2 The Pastoral Function in Christian Education . 117

3.3 The Consequences of Extended Leadership 118

3.4 Religion, State and 'Sovereign Democracy' In Putin's Russia 120

3.5 Russia's Regime Change Won't Cause Pandemonium or Collapse 149

3.6 The implications of Xi Jinping's third term for the world 156

3.7 The one-man rule is back 158

3.8 Islamic View like The Shura on Power Transfer with Refernce from the Qua'ran and Hadidth 161

3.9 Islam's View of Government Leadership Rotation: A Comparative Study of China and Russia 166

3.10 China and Xi Jinping 169

3.11 Argument in Favor of Regular Leadership Changes 171

3.12 Obstacles and Things to Think About............ 173

3.13 Political Aspect of Islam with View on Power Transfer... 175

3.14 The Islamic Perspective on Democracy: Examining the Hadith and Quran with an Indian Case Study 178

3.16 Difficulties and Rebuttals: 182

3.17 A Jewish View of Governance Transition: Analysing Putin and Xi Jinping's Positions in China and Russia... 184

3.18 Reforming Government: A Jewish Necessity .. 188

3.19 Hinduism View 189

Chapter Four: Power Transition Perspective in India; a Case Study of Narendra Modi 196

4.1 The Decline Of India's Democratic System 196

4.2 What democracy means. 199

4.3 Possibility of preserving Indian democracy? 217

4.4 The history of Narendra Modi in the history of India's Politics.. 219

4.5 The Controversial Use of Central Agencies in India: N. Modi's Government and Its Alleged Pressure on Political Opponents............................... 223

4.6 Case Studies and Examples................................. 228

4.7 Implications and Concerns.................................. 230

4. 8The Government's Perspective 231

4.9 Possible Reform Strategies....................................232

4.10 The Negative Impacts of Narendra Modi's Extended Tenure in Governance in India and the Significance of Leadership Transition......................235

4.11 The significance of leadership transitions........240

Chapter Five: Conclusion 243

References 255

Chapter One

Introduction

1.1 Background and Justification

A country's history, socioeconomic progress, and protection of citizen rights and interests are all significantly influenced by its government. The idea of government has taken many different shapes throughout human history, from autocracies and monarchs to democracies and republics. No matter the format, the question of how long a government should hold power is nonetheless important and frequently divisive. In this study, we analyze the intricacies and nuanced issues surrounding the question of why government should change after a specific period of time.

Regular government change is not a novel concept. Societies have struggled with the idea of changing leaders and the need to put a time limit on how long a government can rule for throughout history. From prehistoric societies to contemporary democracies, this concept has changed and taken on various forms. Regular government change is supported for a variety of reasons, all of which are firmly anchored in the ideas of democracy, accountability, and sound governance. Although there are strong arguments in its favor, there are also reservations due to possible difficulties, such as the requirement for stability and continuity in governance.

A nation's government or leader changes, bringing about political change. This could happen frequently or only once every few decades, depending on the nation. Furthermore, not every political shift is beneficial. With respect to Congress, state governments, and presidential terms that alternate every four to eight years, political change in the US occurs almost continuously. Nonetheless, this political shift does not jeopardize the stability of the United States since its citizens have enjoyed this type of democracy for more than 200 years. In actuality, the nation can benefit from these political shifts and become more representative of the people's will.

On the other hand, some nations undergo frequent political upheaval, which causes instability in those nations. Since some nations have not had the chance to experience democracy for hundreds of years, it is simpler for politicians to create new constitutions and continually reorganize their governments, or for military leaders to seize power.

Political change is not always good and can even originate from outside the nation; however, it can frequently result in positive change within a nation.

From a political perspective, during the time frame examined by the study, all of these nations experienced a change in government. Specifically, the Labor government led the United Kingdom in 2008; Gordon Brown had been the prime minister since June 2007. Following the general election in May 2010, Conservative Party leader David Cameron forged a coalition government with the

Liberal Democrats that remains in power as of this writing.

Regarding France, a semi-presidential republic, Nicolas Sarkozy, a member of the conservative Union for a Popular Movement (Union pour un movement Populaire), served as president from May 16, 2007, to May 15, 2012. During that time, he nominated François Fillon to lead the government as prime minister. Following the universal suffrage direct election, Socialist Party leader François Hollande took office as president on May 15, 2012, and named Jean-Marc Ayrault as prime minister. Ayrault was succeeded as prime minister on March 31, 2014, by Manuel Valls.

José Zapatero (Partido Socialista Obrero Español, PSOE) led a socialist government in Spain in 2008 and was reelected to a second term in office. Following the 2011 election, the People's Party (Partido Popular) led by the Center-Right Popular Party secured a majority and formed a government. Mariano Rajoy, who had led the opposition under the Zapatero administrations, served as prime minister.

Regarding Italy, Silvio Berlusconi, the head of the center-right People of Freedom (Popolo della Libertà) party, formed a coalition government following the 2008 general election. The difficult economic climate and internal scandals forced him to step down in 2011.

President of the Republic Giorgio Napolitano nominated Mario Monti to lead a technocratic government that lasted until a new election in February 2013 and the inauguration of a new administration headed by Enrico

Letta in April of that same year. Matteo Renzi succeeded Enrico Letta as prime minister on February 22, 2014.

We will discuss the historical background of government tenure, examine the arguments in favour of term limits, and give a summary of the main issues and goals of this study. This research aims to clarify the complex dynamics of government transition and offer insights into the variables that need to be taken into account when deciding whether, when, and how to change governments.

1.2 Area and Restrictions

Temporal and Geographic Scope

In order to give our analysis a clear framework, it is imperative that we define the scope of our study. Governments all over the world can use the universal concept of government tenure. However, we will mainly concentrate on democratic and semi-democratic systems for the purposes of this study. This covers both developed and developing countries, as well as those with parliamentary or presidential systems of government. It is significant to remember that different governance models might have special characteristics and factors to take into account. We will address these variations as needed.

In addition, we will take into account both historical and modern examples to extract lessons from various eras. This will enable us to analyse how ideas and practises surrounding government tenure have changed over time and to take into account the ways in which different societies have dealt with this problem. Cases classified as historical will feature prominent instances from antiquated societies, and cases classified as contemporary will feature nations that have imposed term limits in the modern era.

Restrictions and Limitations

Despite its goal of comprehensiveness, this research has certain limitations. The accessibility and dependability of data and sources is one major limitation. The research will primarily draw from extant literature, official documents, and professional judgements.

There might be differences in the completeness and accuracy of these sources, as well as access restrictions to certain official records or confidential data.

The inherent subjectivity and erratic nature of term limit application is another drawback. Depending on cultural, political, and historical factors, governmental changes may or may not be appropriate or effective in a given nation. As such, the research will endeavour to offer a comprehensive comprehension while recognising that particular circumstances might demand distinct resolutions.

1.3 Methods: Design of Research

This study will use a mixed-methods approach to effectively address the research questions and objectives. In order to present a comprehensive understanding of the topic, it will include both qualitative and quantitative analyses. To comprehend the historical development of government tenure and the subtleties of its application, qualitative approaches will be employed, such as content analysis of historical documents and interviews with specialists in governance and political science. The impact of governmental change on a range of societal indicators, including political stability, economic development, and levels of corruption, will be evaluated through the application of quantitative methods, such as data analysis and statistical modelling.

Methods of Data Collection

A thorough examination of academic journals, books, and official government records pertaining to government tenure will be part of the data gathering process. We will also interview experts in the field, including political scientists, historians, and policymakers. For the quantitative analysis, survey data and historical records will be utilised. In addition, case studies of nations with and without term limits will be looked at in order to give examples and context from the actual world.

Methods of Data Analysis

There will be both qualitative and quantitative methods used in data analysis. The methods of content analysis and thematic coding will be used to examine the qualitative data. We will find patterns and recurrent themes in policy documents, expert opinions, and historical accounts.

Methods of Data Collection

A thorough examination of academic journals, books, and official government records pertaining to government tenure will be part of the data gathering process. We will also interview experts in the field, including political scientists, historians, and policymakers. For the quantitative analysis, survey data and historical records will be utilised. In addition, case studies of nations with and without term limits will be looked at in order to give examples and context from the actual world.

1.4 Setting Up the Research

Fve main chapters, including this introduction and a conclusion, will make up this study. The historical perspective on government tenure, the advantages of frequent government change, the reasons against frequent government change, case studies of government tenure, and a conclusion outlining the main conclusions, suggested policies, and implications for future governance will all be covered in the ensuing chapters.

In order to comprehend the beginnings of government and the development of governance models, Chapter 2 will take us on a historical tour on the roman and Pasian history. study's

We will examine how various societies have viewed the idea of a change in leadership and how it affects governance.

Chapter three will take deep research on Putin and Jinping long stay of power in Russia and China respectively, their negative impact and why there should be power transfer from one to another.

Chapter four will be focus on N. Modi's era in India, the negative effects, how he is using agencies to pressurize his opponent and why there should be power shift the last chapter, will offer a summary of the major conclusions, go over the research questions again, and offer policy recommendations. It will also go over how government is changing in the modern world and what that means for governance in the future.

We hope that this exploration will advance the conversation about the length of government and how it affects countries. This study aims to offer a comprehensive understanding of this crucial issue and its implications for modern governance by examining the historical background, advantages, and difficulties of frequent government change. In the end, we hope to provide insightful analysis of the ongoing discussion about why governments should change at specific intervals and to offer direction to scholars, policymakers, and citizens in their quest of effective and accountable governance.

Chapter Two

Romanand Parsian History and the Transfer of Power in Human History

In human history and governance, the notion of shifting power from one person or group to another is essential. Power transfer dynamics have moulded civilizations, empires, and countries, frequently leading to profound changes and metamorphoses. Using the rich tapestry of Roman history as our case study, we will examine how the idea of transferring power evolved throughout human history in this 2000-word account. We will examine the intricate and varied process of transferring power and the lessons it teaches modern societies, drawing on a variety of sources such as historical writings, philosophical treatises, and academic analyses.

2.1 Early Concepts of Governance and Power

The earliest forms of social organisation and governance are where the idea of power transfer in human societies originated. In the past, the idea of divine authority was frequently closely associated with the exercise of power. Leaders and rulers were seen as go-betweens between the gods and the mortal world, and religious or mythological stories served to justify their authority.

Mesopotamia is home to one of the oldest known power transfer systems, dating back to 3000 BCE, when the Sumerians established a kingship tradition. Power was passed down through this system from one king to the next, frequently in a hereditary framework, underscoring the significance of dynastic continuity. Although it was not without difficulties and disputes as various power centres within the society fought for influence, this practice served as an early model for how power could be transferred within a society.

The influence of Greece

Influential in the development of political philosophy and thought, the Greek city-states were a major influence on the idea of power transfer. Specifically, the political theories of Aristotle and Plato have had a long-lasting influence on the development of government and the transfer of power.

In "The Republic," Plato developed the idea of the philosopher-king and argued in favour of the wisest and most moral people ruling. The concept that power should ideally be given to those who are most qualified to use it for the good of society was established by this idea, even though it may not seem to have anything to do with power transfer. Plato's conception of a just ruler introduced the notion that merit and virtue ought to be factors in the distribution of power, marking a dramatic break from the hereditary model.

In his work "Politics," Aristotle, on the other hand, advanced our understanding of the virtues and shortcomings of different political systems, such as democracies, aristocracies, and monarchies. Later political theorists who debated the issue of how power should be distributed and the most just type of government were influenced by this philosophical investigation of governance, which also helped shape the discussions surrounding the transfer of power.

2.2 Roman Republic: A Power Transfer Case Study

A fascinating case study on the transfer of power is the Roman Republic. A sophisticated system of checks and balances, which distributed power among the Senate, consuls, and other magistrates, served as the cornerstone of the early Roman Republic. The regular transfer of authority and the division of power acted as a model for later republican systems, like the US.

A fundamental tenet of the Roman Republic was the yearly election of magistrates, which comprised tribunes, praetors, and consuls. These individuals were in charge of enforcing the law and running the state. Regular elections and stringent term limits prevented a single person or group from holding a disproportionate amount of power over time.

Moreover, the Roman Republic was a prime example of the imperium principle, which confers authority upon magistrates. The imperium was not inherited; rather, it was bestowed for a set period of time, which constrained the authority of any one person. In order to prevent anyone from establishing a long-lasting autocracy, this method of power transfer promoted the notion that leadership should be transient.

There were difficulties in the Roman Republic, as the battle between the plebeians and the patricians demonstrated. Representing the common people, the plebeians called for increased political participation and rights. The Twelve Tables, a body of legislation that established the cornerstone of Roman legal thought, were the result of this struggle. The plebeians' struggles and demands for more representation in the government served as a reminder of how power transfer is understood and how important it is for a wider range of people to participate in governance.

2.3 The Roman Republic's Decline

Understanding the shift in power throughout human history requires an understanding of the fall of the Roman Republic and the rise of the Roman Empire. Rome's transition from a republic to an empire offers important lessons about the frailty of political structures and the effects of unbridled power.

Julius Caesar's ascent to power was one of the most significant periods in Roman history. His appointment as dictator for life in 44 BCE and his crossing of the Rubicon River in 49 BCE both signalled a dramatic break from the conventional Roman model of power transfer. The rise of Caesar brought to light the perils of individual ambition and the deterioration of Republican values. Senators who feared the collapse of the Republic planned his assassination in 44 BCE, illustrating the extent to which some were prepared to go in order to maintain the status quo.

Rome went through a period of political unrest and civil wars after Caesar's murder. Stabilising the Roman state was the goal of the Second Triumvirate, which included Lepidus, Mark Antony, and Octavian (Augustus). But in the end, the coalition fell apart, and Octavian became the only emperor. As he assumed the title of "Augustus" in 27 BCE, he essentially became the first Roman Emperor, and his rise to power signalled the end of the Roman Republic and the beginning of the Roman Empire.

The shift from a republic to an empire was not without its challenges and disagreements. While many of the institutions of the restored Republic were preserved under Augustus's careful maintenance of the façade, he was ultimately in charge. A new model of power transfer was established by the Roman Empire, whereby emperors were frequently chosen by adoption as opposed to hereditary succession. This made it possible to choose heirs who were deemed capable of upholding the stability of the empire.

2.4 Roman Empire and Its Successors

With its enormous territory and heterogeneous populace, the Roman Empire was constantly confronted with the issue of power transfer. The succession plan that emperors established had to guarantee the empire's stability and continuity. The designation of a designated heir, frequently through adoption or marriage, was the most popular method of succession.

Adopting successors was a crucial practice in guaranteeing the accession of deserving individuals to the throne. One prominent instance is Nerva's adoption of Trajan, which epitomised the principle that authority ought to be delegated to those who possess the skills and knowledge necessary to rule successfully. Because the best candidate was chosen on the basis of their qualifications and virtues rather than their birthright, this approach to succession was guided by the principle of merit.

In addition, the concept of the "Five Good Emperors"—Hadrian, Trajan, Marcus Aurelius, Antoninus Pius, and Nerva—during the second century of the common era emphasised the advantages of a well-organised and largely stable handover of power. These emperors placed a high value on the wellbeing of the empire and the necessity of governing justly. Their ability to smoothly transition power, frequently through adoption, served as a template for dynasties and governments in the future.

2.5 Experienced a Crisis Characterised by Frequent Military Takeovers, Usurpations, and Assassinations.

The fall of the Roman Empire demonstrated how difficult it is to sustain efficient power transfers over time, especially in a large empire under pressure from both the inside and the outside. The concept of merit-based succession began to crumble as instability increased, and military emperors who frequently usurped power by force emerged throughout the empire.

The empire was further weakened by political division, an economic downturn, and barbarian incursions. A centuries-long superpower came to an end in 476 CE with the fall of the Western Roman Empire. A clear illustration of what happens when power transfer is not managed well and fundamental problems in a political system are not addressed is the fall of the Western Roman Empire.

Lessons from the History of Rome

There are many important lessons that modern societies and governments can learn from the study of Roman history and the transfer of power.

1. The Significance of Merit-Based Leadership: The Roman Republic and Empire served as examples of the advantages of choosing leaders based on qualifications and merit as opposed to inherited lineage. More stability and more efficient governance may result from this strategy.

2. Checks and balances: The Roman Republic's system of checks and balances, which distributes authority among several institutions, serves as an example of how crucial it is to avoid the concentration of power in the hands of one person or organisation. It is possible to prevent the abuse of power with a well-designed system of governance.

3. Crisis Management: The fall of the Roman Empire offers a sobering lesson in the consequences of ineffectively handling both internal and external crises. To preserve stability, governments need to be flexible and sensitive to changing circumstances.

4. Public Participation: The plebeians' calls for increased involvement in politics underscore the significance of wide-ranging political inclusion. Political structures that are inclusive can aid in averting social unrest and advancing the legitimacy of the state.

5. The Dynamic Nature of Power: The history of Rome demonstrates how power transfers are dynamic processes that change over time. Governments and societies alike must be adaptable to the shifting demands and conditions of the world.

Over the course of human civilization, the idea of shifting power from one person or group to another has evolved into a sophisticated and lengthy historical phenomenon. The case study of Roman history, from the early Republic to the Roman Empire, offers important insights into the opportunities and problems associated with the transfer of power. Modern governments and societies can benefit from the lessons learned from the Roman experience, which include the importance of merit-based leadership, checks and balances, crisis management, public participation, and the dynamic nature of power.

While societies continue to struggle with the issue of distributing power in a fair and effective manner, historical analysis, especially the lessons learned from the ascent and

The fall of Rome can influence governmental choices and strategies, guaranteeing that the transfer of power continues to be a vital component of stability and advancement in human societies.

2.6 A Case Study of the Roman Kingdom on the Development of Power Transfer

Throughout human civilization's history, the idea of transferring power from one person to another has been essential. Gaining an understanding of the origins and evolution of this practice is essential to understanding the evolution of political systems. We will go into the early history of the Roman Kingdom, following its path from legendary beginnings to the establishment of a monarchy and how it ultimately cleared the path for the formation of a republic, in order to investigate the roots of power transfer. A fascinating case study is provided by the evolution of power transfer within the framework of the Roman Kingdom, which illuminates the factors that contributed to the shift from monarchical to more democratic forms of government.

1. Rome's Mythological Origins

Roman mythology, of which the most well-known story is that of Romulus and Remus, is a major source of information about the founding of Rome. These twin brothers were raised by a she-wolf after being abandoned as babies, according to legend. When they got older, they made the decision to found a city in their hometown, but a disagreement over who should lead it ultimately resulted in the creation of Rome. In 753 BCE, driven by ambition, Romulus killed his brother Remus to become Rome's first king (Tainter, 1988). Important concepts of power transfer are introduced in the founding myth of Rome, most notably the notion of a single person assuming authority via force and ambition.

2.7 Roman Monarchy: An Historical Overview

A monarchy, in which the king had total authority over the state, was a defining feature of the early Roman Empire. From father to son, the kingship was a hereditary institution, and the king was frequently seen as a political and religious leader. In the early Roman state, his function as a priest-king was emphasised, and his authority came from divine favour. The transfer of power during this period was based on monarchy and was mostly familial and hereditary, making it noteworthy.

The Influence of Etruscan

The Etruscans, a highly developed civilization in northern Italy, had a significant influence on the early Roman Kingdom. The Etruscans are thought to have had a major influence on the development of early Roman political structures and the introduction of the idea of monarchy. The Etruscans were the source of many elements of the Roman monarchy, including the emblem of the king's authority and specific administrative procedures (Cornell, 1995). The dynamics of power transfer in the Roman Kingdom were impacted by this outside force.

Power Transfer and the Monarchic System

Hereditary succession was the main method of power transfer in the early Roman Kingdom. The son of the reigning monarch, whether biological or adopted, would take over and maintain the royal line of succession. This system did not, however, come without difficulties. In order to justify their rule, kings were expected to uphold their relationship with God, and any indication that they were incapable or that God was not pleased with them could result in their overthrow. In these situations, the Senate—which is made up of the most influential nobility—would be crucial in approving the overthrow and installation of a new monarch (Forsythe, 2005).

Even though it was supposedly hereditary, this system of power transfer included elements of aristocratic approval, demonstrating an early example of checks and balances within the monarchy. In order to maintain the balance of power and give legitimacy to the transfer of power, the aristocracy was indispensable.

The Monarchy's Boundaries

Similar to other monarchies, the Roman Kingdom was not without its limitations. Tensions within the aristocracy frequently resulted from the king's unbridled power as they attempted to limit the monarch's authority. When a king demonstrated autocratic traits or behaved contrary to the aristocracy's interests, these tensions were heightened. This dynamic is best illustrated by the legend of the final Roman king, Lucius Tarquinius Superbus.

Tarquin the Proud, also known as Lucius Tarquinius Superbus, was a despotic ruler whose harsh reign ultimately resulted in his overthrow. His autocratic actions, such as the rape of a noblewoman named Lucretia, infuriated the nobility. Ancient historians such as Livy (in "The History of Rome") have described this event, which emphasises the growing dissatisfaction with monarchical rule. Tarquin the Proud's tale serves as an example of how an overabundance of power concentrated in the hands of one person can cause people to reject monarchical authority and yearn for a different kind of government.

When the Roman Republic was founded

The Roman Republic was established as a result of a significant political transformation brought about by the discontent with Tarquin's rule. After Tarquin's expulsion in 509 BCE, the Roman nobility, under the leadership of individuals such as Lucius Junius Brutus, made the decision to do away with the monarchy and establish a new, more equitable form of government. With the introduction of an elected government and a system of checks and balances, the Roman Republic represented a dramatic break from the hereditary monarchy of the early kingdom (Beard, North, & Price, 1998).

A turning point in the development of power transfer occurred with the establishment of the Roman Republic. It signalled the change from an inherited monarchy to a more open-minded and democratic political structure. A number of elected political positions, including senators and consuls, that were rotated on a regular basis by the populace defined the Roman Republic. This signalled a significant shift in the distribution of power within Roman society.

2.8 The Roman Republic's Mechanisms for Power Transfer

A number of power-transfer mechanisms were introduced by the Roman Republic, breaking with the monarchical tradition. Among these mechanisms were the following ones:

1. Consuls: There were two consuls in the Roman Republic who were elected annually and shared executive authority. Their one-year tenure made sure that power was transferred regularly and under control. The consulship

was established to stop any one person from gaining undue influence.

2. Senate: Made up of ageing statesmen, the Roman Senate was essential in advising and swaying political decisions. The Senate as an institution offered continuity and stability in government, and senators were appointed for life.

3. Popular Assemblies: A number of popular assemblies gave the public a voice in making decisions, especially when it came to enacting legislation and choosing representatives. This Roman Republic feature promoted more inclusive forms of government.

4. Term Limits: In order to prevent any one person from holding office indefinitely, many offices in the Roman Republic had term limits. This was a conscious effort to prevent the consolidation of power.

Rome Teaches Us About the Development of Power Transfer

The Roman Kingdom-Roman Republic transition offers important insights into the evolution of power transfer and the factors that shaped this transition. From the Roman experience, several important lessons can be learned:

1. A Reaction to Monarchical Excess: Tarquin the Proud's and other monarchs' excesses contributed to the move away from monarchy. It emphasized the need for checks and balances and the perils of consolidating power in the hands of one person.

2. External Influences: The adoption of some political institutions in early Rome was influenced by the Etruscans. This illustrates how outside influences can influence how a society's power transfer mechanisms evolve.

3. Aristocratic Involvement: The aristocracy played a crucial role in both the monarchy and the republic. They could influence the succession in a monarchy by endorsing or disapproving of the king's rule. They took an active part in state governance in the republic.

4. Transition to More Inclusive Systems: The Roman Republic's founding was a major step towards the development of a more inclusive and democratic system of governance. The introduction of mechanisms, like popular assemblies and elected officials, signified a break from the hereditary monarchy.

5. Halving Stability and Change: The Roman Republic served as an example of how to combine stability and change in a harmonious way. In order to facilitate a seamless transition, it kept some stable components, like the Senate, even as it instituted new power transfer mechanisms.

An intriguing case study of the evolution of the idea of power transfer in antiquity is the history of the Roman Kingdom and its transition into the Roman Republic. The shift from monarchy to republicanism was not a smooth one; rather, it was a reaction to the problems presented by excessive monarchy, outside forces, and the need for a more equitable and inclusive system of government.

The Roman experience teaches us important things about the dynamics of power relations in human societies. It emphasises the value of checks and balances, the role played by outside forces, the aristocracy's influence, and the necessity of striking a balance between political systems' need for stability and change.

The principles of power transfer and governance established during the early years of the Roman Republic continued to shape the course of Roman history and have an impact on later political developments in the Western world, even though the Roman Republic eventually gave way to the Roman Empire. The Roman case study offers a wealth of information regarding the development of power relations and the ongoing pursuit of a more just and equitable form of government.

2.9 Power Transfer Evolution: Insights from the Roman Republic

In the history of human civilization, the idea of power transfer from one person or entity to another has been crucial. One essential tenet of democratic societies is the notion that no one individual or group should be able to exercise absolute power for an extended period of time. We look to the Roman Republic, a society that had a significant impact on the evolution of contemporary political systems, to investigate the roots of this idea. The history of the Roman Republic and the concepts it advanced regarding the distribution of power will be covered in this essay. Further historical and scholarly sources will be consulted in order to present a thorough examination of the development of this important idea.

1. When the Roman Republic Began

When the Roman populace rebelled against King Tarquin's autocratic rule in 509 BCE, the Roman Republic rose from the ashes of the Roman Kingdom. During this time, a more representative and participatory form of government replaced the monarchy. The Roman Republic was not an isolated event; it was influenced by various Greek and Etruscan political ideas and institutions. Historian Polybius observed, "In place of one-man rule, they [the Romans] established a more balanced and equitable form of government." (Polybius, "Histories," Book 6, 1.1).

One of the main features of the Roman Republic was its intricate system of checks and balances. It included a separation of powers between the Senate, the magistrates, and the popular assemblies, among other branches. The idea that political power should be shared among the ruling class rather than concentrated in the hands of one person emerged during this period as one of the fundamental concepts. This was partially a response to the despotism of the Roman emperors, but it was also impacted by Greek political theory, especially the works of Aristotle and other scholars.

2. The Impact of Greece on the Roman Republic

The political theories of the Greeks were not lost on the architects of the Roman Republic, which did not arise in a vacuum. In his treatise "Politics," Aristotle examined various systems of governance and the idea of power rotation. Aristotle stated in "Politics," Book 4, 1290a, "It is in the nature of a democracy that, since the generality of persons are free and not well-off, the poor have more power than the rich." This idea of a rotation of power to prevent the tyranny of a single class found resonance in Rome.

Roman political thought was greatly influenced by Aristotle's writings, particularly the notion that power shouldn't be permanently vested in one class or group. By incorporating this idea into their political structure, the Romans made sure that different institutions and social classes shared authority. For example, the Roman Senate was an aristocratic body tasked with advising the magistrates and directing the Republic's policies. Senators were appointed based on their standing and qualifications rather than being elected. This served as a means of transferring power between the aristocratic generations in and of itself.

3. Cin Cinnabon and the Righteous Ruler

Lucius Quinctius Cincinnatus was one of the most famous characters in Roman history and a prime example of the concept of power transfer. A farmer named Cincinatus was called upon to rule as a dictator during difficult times. The Senate created the post of dictator as a temporary measure to handle crises. After taking on the position, Cincinatus would have almost total authority, but only for a limited time and for a clear objective. When the crisis passed, he was supposed to give up his power.

The deeds of Cincinatus represented the Roman conception of benevolent autocracy and the voluntary ceding of power. In contemporary times, George Washington is frequently likened to Caesar for his willingness to transfer power, having given up his leadership of the Continental Army and refusing to ascend to the throne.

4. The Collegiality Concept in Roman Law

A system of collegiality, which was also used in the Roman Republic, is thought to have predated the concept of a balance of power as it exists today. Two people held some positions at a time, such as the two consuls who functioned as the highest-ranking executive officials. The purpose of this system was to keep any one individual from becoming overly powerful. It embodied the idea of shared power because it compelled the consuls to cooperate and come to a consensus when they disagreed.

Collegiality was a deeply ingrained practice in Roman politics that held that no one should have absolute power for an extended length of time. As Polybius put it in his "Histories," "The Roman constitution provided an admirable balance between monarchy, aristocracy, and democracy." (Polybius, "Histories," Book 6, 11.8) The division of authority among several officials served as a deterrent to despotism and as an early example of the concept that power ought to be shared among various leaders.

The Republican Ideal and Cicero

The late Republic era, which was marked by political unrest and civil unrest, was the height of the Roman Republic. Cicero, the well-known orator, philosopher, and statesman, was one of the important individuals of this time. Cicero was a fervent supporter of constitutional government and the Republican ideal. In "De Re Publica," he elaborated on the idea of power transfer and the significance of checks and balances in government.

In his writings, Cicero stressed the importance of upholding the Republic and the need to defend it against those who would try to upset the balance of power. Cicero's contributions to political thought highlighted the Roman commitment to the idea that a republic's longevity and health depended on a rotation of power and the preservation of its institutions. He wrote, "The state is one great whole. It can never be preserved if one part of it is mutilated or infected with disease." (Cicero, "De Re Publica," Book 2, 3.4).

Slippage and Convergence

Eventually, the Roman Republic experienced a period of decline characterised by social unrest, power struggles, and corruption. The traditional Republican principles started to erode as the wealth gap between the rich and the poor grew. The ascent of formidable military leaders like Pompey, Crassus, and Julius Caesar heralded a break from the established Roman political structure. Like the autocratic rulers the Republic had once rejected, these leaders aspired to amass power.

The fall of the Republic and the Roman Empire served as a stark reminder of how brittle the concept of power transfer is and how easily it can be undermined by zealous individuals. It also demonstrated how crucial it is to uphold Roman Republic ideals in order to guarantee the ongoing transfer of power.

History and Significance

The idea of power transfer has been greatly influenced by the Roman Republic and continues to have a lasting influence on political philosophy. It established the foundation for contemporary democratic ideas and the idea that no person or organisation should have unrestricted power forever.

For example, the Roman Republic served as a source of inspiration for the American Founding Fathers as they created the country's political structure. The checks and balances of the Roman Republic are mirrored in the U.S. Constitution, which establishes a division of power among the legislative, executive, and judicial branches. The Roman notion of power transfer is the source of the notion of term limits for public office holders, which is a fundamental component of contemporary democracies.

The development of the Roman Republic and its ultimate union with the Roman Empire provide important new perspectives on the idea of power transfer. This historical era illustrated the significance of maintaining checks and balances in order to protect a republic's health and the need to avoid the concentration of power. These ideas were developed with the help of Roman political figures such as Cicero, who were influenced by Greek political philosophy. Even though internal conflict and avaricious leaders ultimately brought about the Republic's downfall, its legacy endured and had a significant impact on the establishment of contemporary democracies.

A historical point of reference for comprehending the origins of this important concept is the Roman Republic's dedication to the concept of power transfer, as demonstrated by individuals such as Cincinnatus, the practice of collegiality, and the writings of Cicero. A monument to the Roman civilization's lasting influence on political philosophy and practice worldwide, the ideas of the Roman Republic still serve as a source of inspiration and guidance for discussions on modern governance.

2.10 A Historical View of the Development of Power Transfer Using the Roman Empire

Over the ages, the idea of power shifting from one ruler or ruling body to another has significantly shaped human history and governmental systems. Numerous social, political, and cultural factors have shaped this idea. We need to study the history books and make use of the Roman Empire as a point of reference in order to comprehend how this concept got ingrained in the human psyche. With its intricate political structure and succession plan, the Roman Empire offers an insightful case study for examining the development of power dynamics. This essay will look at the mechanisms employed in the Roman Empire, the historical foundations of power transfer, and the ways in which these concepts are still relevant in contemporary political systems.

1. The History of Power Transmission

The earliest human societies are whence the idea of power transference originated. Historians and anthropologists have noted that even in ancient tribes, election, merit, and heredity were frequently used to select leaders. These techniques changed over time as a result of societal, political, and cultural factors. Power dynamics evolved along with the complexity of societies.

1. Biological Succession

Hereditary succession, in which leadership within a ruling family was passed down from generation to generation, was one of the first forms of power transfer. Power transmission of this kind was common in prehistoric societies such as Egypt, Mesopotamia, and China. Hereditary leadership within some noble families was also a practice in the Roman Republic, which existed before the Roman Empire.

Elective Courses

Certain societies had elective systems for the transfer of power, in which leaders were chosen on the basis of their qualifications or with the approval of a council or assembly. An important example of a civilization that adopted an early form of democracy, in which citizens elected officials, is ancient Athens. Later, the evolution of contemporary representative democracies would be influenced by this idea of elective power transfers.

US military invasion

Military commanders have always been important players in the transfer of power. They would usurp the current rulers by using force to seize power. Particularly during the Roman Empire, there were numerous instances of military commanders—typically generals—taking over as rulers. In ancient Rome, this kind of power transfer was typical and would continue to influence the organization of the empire's government.

Authority Distribution in the Roman Republic

With its existence spanning from 509 BC to 27 BC, the Roman Republic offers important insights into the earliest forms of power sharing. The Roman Republic was distinguished by a sophisticated form of government that included a Senate and elected officials. Rome's power structure during this time was complex, influenced by both merit and heredity.

1. The Roman Senate and Consuls

As the highest authority in the state, the Roman Republic's two consuls, who were elected every year, held the majority of power. These consuls were chosen using a mix of elective and hereditary processes. Although candidates for consulships had to belong to the senatorial class, they were nevertheless chosen by Roman citizens, albeit under certain limitations.

In contrast, the members of the Roman Senate were appointed for life. Although they mainly served as advisors, they had a big say in political choices. The Senate acted as a storehouse of knowledge and authority, facilitating the orderly transition of power.

The Honorific Cursus

In order to advance to the rank of consul or other high office in the Roman Republic, one had to follow the Cursus Honorum, a meticulously planned career path. Aspiring politicians had to hold a series of positions, both military and civil, according to the Cursus Honorum in order to qualify for the consulship. This system was put in place to make sure that people running for important positions had proven their allegiance to the Roman government and gained the required experience.

Superb Transfers of Authority

The Roman Republic saw many power battles and disputes, but it also saw some extraordinary handoffs of authority. The appointment of dictators during emergency situations is one prominent example. Temporary and extraordinary powers were granted to dictators to deal with emergencies; after the crisis passed, they were expected to resign from office. This practice demonstrates how adaptable Roman political structures were to the transfer of power.

The Roman Empire's Transition

In the end, the Roman Republic gave way to the Roman Empire, which represented a dramatic change in the distribution of power. The Roman Empire had centralised, autocratic rule and lasted from 27 BC to 476 AD (the Eastern Roman Empire continued to exist until 1453).

1. Augustus's and the Principate's Roles

When Augustus (formerly Octavian) took the throne as the first Roman Emperor in 27 BC, it made the shift from the Roman Republic to the Roman Empire easier. Augustus instituted the Principate, a governance structure that preserved the characteristics of the Republic while consolidating authority within the Emperor's hands. Augustus had extraordinary authority known as imperium, which gave him the ability to command the legions and effectively govern the Roman state, even though he was officially holding offices like consul. This signified a profound change in the Roman understanding of power dynamics.

Contingent Succession

Throughout the Roman Empire, the custom of hereditary succession persisted. Numerous emperors designated their heirs as co-rulers or adopted well-known people as their heirs. For instance, the Julio-Claudian dynasty produced a number of blood- or adoption-related emperors, such as Tiberius, Caligula, Claudius, and Nero. For centuries to come, emperors would consistently train members of their inner circle or family to be their successors.

A Crisis and an Assault

There were also many examples of military usurpation of power throughout the Roman Empire. Particularly in the third century, military uprisings and outside threats caused frequent changes of emperors. The idea of "barracks emperors" developed, in which military leaders from various provinces would acclaim themselves as emperors and attempt to seize power. Due to these crises, the dynamics of power transfer changed, with the military becoming an important factor in deciding who led.

The Roman Empire's Influence on Contemporary Theories of Power Transfer

Modern governance systems are still influenced by the power-transfer practices and ideas of the Roman Empire. Power dynamics in modern societies have been profoundly influenced by a number of aspects of Roman governance.

1. The Imperium Concept

Modern conceptions of executive power have been influenced by the idea of imperium, which signifies the power to lead the legions and rule the state. Heads of state and government in modern democracies and republics frequently have a great deal of power and are granted comparable authority to Roman emperors, but within a system of checks and balances.

The Senate's and Advisers' Legacy

Modern governments still use variations of the Roman Senate and the concept of advisers. Senates, upper houses, or councils are places where leaders receive advice from knowledgeable people and engage in deliberation. These organisations are essential to forming public policy and maintaining the integrity of the government.

Democratic and Hereditary Components

Both democratic and hereditary components are commonly found in contemporary governments' systems of power transfer. In constitutionally limited monarchies, like the British monarchy, elected parliaments coexist with hereditary succession. Elective monarchy is also practiced in republics, where the people choose their presidents and prime ministers.

Managing crises and usurpations

The experience of the Roman Empire

Crisis situations and military takeovers have shaped how modern states conceptualise their emergency powers. Constitutions and legal frameworks frequently include provisions for extraordinary situations in which a government can exercise greater authority; this is reminiscent of the Roman practice of installing dictators during severe times.

The concept of power transfer originated in the earliest human societies and has developed over millennia. Understanding the historical evolution of this concept is made easier by examining the Roman Empire and its intricate system of government. The complex organisational frameworks of the Roman Republic, the Roman Empire's establishment, and the imperium, Senate, and crisis management traditions all had an impact on the development of contemporary governance structures. Power transfer has changed over time, from merit and heredity to autocracy and military usurpation. This change is a reflection of how human political institutions have evolved to meet changing needs. The lessons learned from the Roman Empire offer a historical basis for understanding the opportunities and challenges associated with authority and leadership transfers, which is helpful as we navigate the complexities of power transfer in the modern world.

2.11 Political Institutions in the Republic Of Rome

How did Rome become the epicentre of the mightiest empire in antiquity, rising from one of the numerous city-states occupying the Italian peninsula? Rome's early development of political institutions is part of the solution. Rome's political structures proved to be resilient and flexible as it grew in power, enabling it to absorb a wide range of ethnic groups. Roman legend states that the last Roman king was deposed by a group of noblemen in 509 BCE, marking the start of the Republic. Two consuls, who were chosen to hold one-year terms and shared many of the same powers as the king, took the throne from the Roman king. The acts of one consul could be overruled by another or vetoed. The idea behind this change—to prevent any one man from becoming too powerful—was present early in Roman thought and shaped many of Rome's political institutions, even though the office of consul did not exist in its final form until approximately 300 BCE.

Roman political structures mirrored the two classes that made up Roman society: the plebeians, or common people, and the patricians, or wealthy elites. At first, political office and decision-making authority were limited to the patricians. Plebeians, for instance, were prohibited from joining the Roman Senate, an advisory body whose recommendations were seriously considered by the consuls but which lacked the authority to enact laws of its own. Plebeians were not eligible to become senators; a Roman had to have held a political office. But eventually, the plebeians were able to exert more power within the political structure.

Plebeians gained new political positions and were granted access to higher positions, such as consulship, between 494 and 287 BCE. The establishment of voting assemblies and councils increased the plebeians' influence over Roman politics. The final obstacle to Plebeian political engagement was eliminated in 287 BCE when a law was passed that did away with the need for patrician senators to ratify proposed laws before the Plebeian Council could consider them.

With these new arrangements, some people gained wealth and power, but many remained impoverished. The Plebeian Council had actual political clout in Roman politics. Political rights did not result in significant changes, in part because the Comitia Centuriata, the principal voting body that chose consuls and other high-ranking officials, was structured according to wealth. A wealthy Roman's vote carried greater weight than that of a poor one because the wealthy were divided into smaller groups than the poor. Each century, or voting group, had one vote.

How did the Romans restrict the authority of a single man in politics?

In what ways did Roman political systems restrict the power of the impoverished?

Warfare

The voting system was a reflection of the Roman military structure, despite the fact that it might have seemed like a calculated plot to give the wealthy more power. The Comitia Centuriata took its name from the century, which was the standard Roman military unit during the kingdom and most of the republican era. Literally, a century was a group of 100 soldiers, though in practice the division was never so exact. Due to the requirement that soldiers supply their own gear, men were classified into classes according to their level of wealth. Because only the wealthy could afford fine armour and weapons, the Romans were more proficient fighters. In spite of being the largest class in terms of population, men without property were not allowed to enlist in the military and were assigned to the lowest number of centuries, so they could not vote.

The wealthy had better motivation to be good soldiers and a better sense of what was good policy for Rome, which is partly why the Romans saw no problem with allowing the wealthy to have greater political influence. They also believed that those with the greatest wealth stood to lose the most from Roman defeat.

What was the rationale for creating wealth-based military units?

Foreign affairs and growth

The Romans had no premeditated strategy to establish an empire. Rather, Rome grew as a result of its conflicts with neighbouring kingdoms, city-states, and empires, and it had to find methods to absorb these new lands and people. Not every conquered person was attempted to become a Roman by the Romans. Roman-ruled cities and regions were generally permitted to preserve their pre-existing political and cultural structures. Rome's vanquished adversaries were only required to supply soldiers for Rome's military operations. Being on the winning side of a battle offered Rome's new allies incentives because, in the ancient world, winning a battle meant taking home a portion of the spoils from the conquered.

Roman citizenship was extended to most defeated enemies, sometimes granting them full voting rights. The expansion of voting rights outside the city limits did not significantly change the political climate in Rome because voting required a physical presence in the city.

Nonetheless, the promise of citizenship did contribute to the development of a common identity centred on allegiance to Rome.

The Romans established formal provinces and appointed former political officeholders to administer them in order to control the new lands that came under their control. Because most provinces were far from Rome, these governors frequently had a great deal of authority and discretion when it came to handling local matters. The Romans made an effort to strike a compromise between granting governors sufficient authority to manage their regions and preventing governors from gaining too much power to pose a threat to Rome's rule.

Why would Rome have granted some degree of citizenship to conquered people?

Financial progress

Rome had to change as its power increased, even though it had little interest in running the day-to-day operations of its friends. Roman roads facilitated the easier and faster movement of both soldiers and goods, thus serving as a means of extending Roman military and economic power. As their power grew, the Romans also produced coins. In 211 BCE, they unveiled the denarius, a tiny silver coin that would later serve as the common currency for the majority of the Roman era.

A common currency promoted trade throughout the expanding Roman Empire. Coins were simple to carry and could be exchanged for any kind of goods or services. The use of currency facilitated resource allocation and relocation, which in turn promoted increased economic activity.

Across the Mediterranean Sea, the Romans conducted trade as well. Since strong political ties were typically a prerequisite for good trade relations, their network of trading contacts grew along with their political influence. Numerous opportunities for economic interactions and growth were created by the military's expansion of protection over a growing territory, road construction, coin minting, and fighting piracy.

Rome's economy, like that of all ancient societies, was centred on labour-intensive agriculture. A large number of small landowners were absent from their homes for extended periods of time as Rome engaged in more foreign wars. In the event that they did not come back or that their farms failed while they were away, affluent Romans purchased their land and built latifundia, or increasingly large farms. Moreover, it was customary to sell war prisoners into slavery, and the growing number of military victories resulted in a large influx of enslaved individuals onto the Italian peninsula. This trend promoted economic production even further because it allowed for economies of scale and allowed enslaved people to work harder and longer hours than free Romans. Development was aided by the increased revenue from expansion, which raised demand for more agricultural products. Small family farms would not have had the option to move from growing staple grains to high-value crops like olives and grapes or raising livestock, as some large farm owners did.

Slaves were frequently purchased by war prisoners. In what way could this practice have linked the economic growth of the Italian peninsula to the Roman military expansion?

Rome's urban development

Rome remained the centre of the empire's political decision-making even as it grew, and the city changed and evolved alongside its empire. In order to maintain a minimal standard of public health, sanitation systems had to be developed for an ever-growing urban population. An early sewer system was created by the Romans in the city. Both the first road, the Via Appia, and the first aqueduct, a structure to transport water over great distances to the city, were constructed in 312 BCE.

Rome was able to finance its construction projects with money gained from its military victories, economic growth, and the ability to collect taxes in currency. The Romans constructed temples and government buildings in addition to aqueducts, roads, and sewers. Triumphant commanders would erect temples honoring specific deities, and they funded these constructions with the spoils they amassed during battles.

Interpreting the Transition from Republic to Principate in Rome, Jurgen Deininger: The fall of the Roman Republic and the establishment of the Principate are unquestionably two of the most important political occurrences in the annals of 'classical' antiquity. Augustus's founding of the Principate is hardly comparable to any brief constitutional and political changes that were commonly encountered, for instance, in the early Greek city states when a tyranny was establishing itself. Events in Rome stood out from many other ancient constitutional changes for at least two reasons: first, the remarkable length and duration of the gradual transformation, which took several generations during its critical phase from the Gracchi to Augustus; second, what could be called the apparent "irreversibility" of this fundamental shift in the Roman political system. The history of the Roman Empire is, in fact, primarily the history of progressively expanding and more sophisticated monarchical government; a return to the previous system of governance did not appear to be feasible.

It is not necessary to go into great detail to prove this here. Thus, it can be concluded that the crisis of the Roman republic and the subsequent shift to monarchy represented a significant and permanent alteration of the political structure, with very few genuine analogues in ancient history. It may also be added that this change from Republic to Principate, or, to put it more broadly, to Monarchy, was generally viewed as a significant negative development and an obvious indication of the demise of the Roman political community, at least in part in antiquity and even more so in modern times. There is no question that the main task of the ancient historian studying the late Roman republic is, and will continue to be, to analyse and describe this large project, Deininger: Explaining the Change from Republic to Principle in Rome, published by BYU ScholarsArchive, 1980, 78, of change at Rome by starting from the innumerable actions and motives of individual leaders and groups. However, it also always seemed necessary to look for the deeper, underlying reasons for this notable disruption in the internal evolution of the Roman state and its institutions. There have been many significant attempts, from Tacitus to Machiavelli, from Montesquieu to contemporary historical research of the 20th century, to comprehend and explain why, despite a plethora of conflicting interests, a great deal of obstinate resistance, and even the personal intentions of numerous political leaders, the ancient Roman republican system was ultimately replaced once and for all by the monarchy. Of course, it would be impossible to provide a thorough account of all these attempts here, especially since no thorough survey of them has ever been done.

Although it would, in my opinion, deepen our understanding of Roman history, there is currently no history of the issue, no methodical analysis, and no comparison of the various answers offered in antiquity or in the present. My goal here, which must be extremely narrow, is to highlight some of the main explanations found mostly in contemporary historical research, try to briefly discuss their merits, and conclude with a few larger historical perspectives and connections that are often but, in my opinion, somewhat unfairly ignored. This essay cannot claim to be the first to explain the vast historical process under discussion in detail, but a cursory review of the relevant literature seems to suggest that efforts to make some points more clear may not be entirely unwelcome or unnecessary. One more preliminary observation is warranted.

It must be acknowledged that, generally speaking, historians focus on other topics and do not consider the issue of underlying causes to be their most important one. As I mentioned earlier in Comparative Civilizations Review, Vol. While underlying causes are treated more by way, it is evident that 4 [1980], No. 4, Art. 5 https://scholarsarchive.byu.edu/ccr/vol4/iss4/5   79 ready, must do so on the analysis of individual events, on the actions and motives of leaders and groups, on the analysis of institutions. I'll give just one example to show you what I mean. The question of the underlying causes of the so-called "Revolution" is virtually avoided in a work as important as Sir Ronald Syme's Roman Revolution, which essentially states that the fundamental issue of the time was the conflict between "liberty" and "political stability": "That was the question confronting the Romans themselves," Sir Ronald says, "and I have tried to answer it precisely in their fashion." However, I'm not sure if this was the issue facing all Romans or just some of them. However, even if one were to agree with Tacitus, for example, there would still be no satisfactory answer to the question of why the Romans faced this conundrum at that precise moment and how urgently.

I will refrain from delving into the historiographic and methodological roots of this mindset. However, despite the significance of "the" Roman perspective for our comprehension of Roman history, it remains debatable if it provides an adequate explanation for the shift from Republic to Monarchy. Even though modern writers address the issue of "causes" explicitly, there are at least two possible approaches to taking it on. The first is listing a number of individual "factors" that have had a significant impact on the shift from a republic to a monarchy (or, as it is often discussed, just the collapse of the republic), without making any attempt to examine the connections between these factors alone or between them and the process of change as a whole. The alternative is the author's own explanation, which is given without a methodical examination of alternative interpretations. 3 Deininger: Explaining the Change from Republic to Principle in Rome, published by BYU ScholarsArchive, 1980. This is undoubtedly closely related to the previously mentioned fact that no attempt has ever been made to create anything approaching a thorough survey of the issue. Of course, the issue at hand has a lengthy past. However, delving into the numerous approaches that have been taken to it since early modern times and in antiquity would be excessive. It must only take a few clues. The well-known "theory of moral decline," which was crucial to Roman self-understanding in the late Republican era, was developed (or appropriated from Greek models) during a point in the crisis when no one realised that monarchy would actually be the solution. Surveying the entire historical process became feasible only during the imperial era, and then the main factors responsible for the shift from Republic to Monarchy were the Civil Wars (which were partly attributed to 'moral decline') and the need for peace; these are essentially the viewpoints presented in the work that Sir Ronald Syme just mentioned. But there is also the argument that, in the end, monarchy was only required because of the size and reach of the Roman Empire.

Tacitus and other authors provide at least a few indications towards this, including some highly intriguing observations made by the jurist Pomponius in his Enchiridium, which was written during Hadrian's reign. All of this warrants a far closer examination than has been done up to this point, and the same is true of the far more elaborate and sophisticated attempts at explanation that date back to the early modern era. I can only bring up J.G.A. Pocock's recent analysis in his Machiavellian Moment here. In a somewhat different context, it is shown in Florentine Political Thought and the Atlantic Republican Tradition, 1975, how Machiavelli saw the citizen militia—as opposed to mercenary soldiers—as the fundamental cornerstone of a Republican constitution, and that, in his opinion, 4 Comparative Civilizations Review, Vol. The fall of the militia and the establishment of a professional army in Rome during the 1980s led to the eventual collapse of the Republic and the establishment of the Monarchy. The same author has noted how, first of all, James Harrington went even farther in 17th-century England by highlighting the republican system's economic foundation, which he believed to be a well-balanced structure of property. It appeared necessary for the Republic to end and the Monarchy to replace it if a sizable portion of the populace lost their property and became economically dependent, if not legally. Then, in the 18th century, Montesquieu was the one who most prominently emphasised the limited connection between the extent of a given territory and its constitution in his Esprit des Lois. He claimed that the three traditional constitutional patterns—monarchy, aristocracy, and democracy—had a counterpart in the trio of extremely large, medium-sized, and tiny territories.

He wasn't the first, by any means, to adopt this viewpoint. Even though David Hume, a younger Scottish contemporary, and others vigorously contested the notion that a Republican constitution could not exist in vastly expanded areas, this theory continued to have a significant impact in certain regions of Europe well after the French Revolution and even into the new century. In his renowned Considerations on the causes of the Romans' greatness and decline, Montesquieu himself devoted a significant amount of space to "moral decline." He summarised the reasons for the Republican system's downfall in Rome with the following formula: "Ce fut uniquement la grandeur de la Republique qui fit son mal," or "It was the very greatness of the Republic that provoked its misfortune." It is evident from the context that "grandeur" refers to the extent of Roman dominance. That concludes our discussion of some of the major historical theories explaining Rome's transition from a republic to a monarchy. Before this essay concludes, we will revisit these theories.

What then becomes of the explanation of the fall of the Roman republic and the genesis of the monarchy in contemporary research, which, incidentally, frequently appears scarcely conscious of the lengthy history of the fundamental issue, 5 Deininger: Explaining the Change from Republic to Principle in Rome, published by BYU ScholarsArchive, 1980-82? I will not list the most significant modern explanations in chronological order because, among other issues, there has never been a structured dialogue between authors that would have provided a pattern for the evolution of contemporary concepts. I would much rather draw a first distinction between theories that, in my opinion, focus too much on peripheral elements of the entire process of change and theories that attempt to explain key elements. While it is obviously impossible to go into detail about all of that here, I believe it is reasonable to draw a distinction between these two kinds of 'explanations'. Even though it can be challenging, I believe that evaluating particular individual factors, as they are highlighted in contemporary literature, involves more than just individual arbitrariness. Let me first make a few observations regarding theories that focus on less important aspects of Rome's transition from Republic to Monarchy.

Since it is obvious that completeness cannot be achieved here, I will only provide four instances of these types of explanations. To sum them up in a nutshell, the Gracchi are primarily responsible for the fall of the Republic and the establishment of the Monarchy in Rome. Second: the massive growth of slavery in Rome and Italy in the second and first centuries B.C. is a social and economic historical phenomenon that is the primary cause of the change in the Roman governmental structure. Thirdly, among theories focusing on secondary aspects, the venerable "theory of moral decay" from antiquity should probably also be included. Lastly, the fourth and most recent interpretation is as follows: In accordance with this understanding, the shift 6 Comparative Civilizations Review, Vol. From Republic to Principate, 4 [1980], No. 4, Art. 5 https://scholarsarchive.byu.edu/ccr/vol4/iss4/5 83 was largely the result of luck combined with some poor choices made by a few prominent Roman statesmen.

Naturally, my point here will not be that none of these theories have any particular value or that they don't help to explain the significant shift that occurred in the Roman world. It must be noted, however, that they are not aiming at the fundamental and important steps that led from a republic to a monarchy.

For example, let's use R.E. as my first example. The author of Smith's 1955 book The Failure of the Roman Republic has upheld the theory that the two Gracchi should bear the primary blame for the fall of the Roman Republic and its consequent consequences. It was they who questioned the Senate's power and leadership role, turning themselves over to the 'mob' (Smith uses this term) as Tiberius did, or, more effectively in his brutally destructive manner, to the equites as Gaius did. Without a doubt, the Gracchi are to blame for the start of the political upheaval in Rome and the initial stages of the crisis. However, it should also be evident that the entire long-term transformational process cannot be adequately explained in terms of the deeds of a small number of prominent figures, whether they be the Gracchi at the beginning or anyone else later on (including the "revolutionary leader" Augustus). This approach to the 'failure of the Roman Republic' has not garnered scholarly support, which is not surprising given that a partial aspect has been exaggerated. Furthermore, it fails to explain the reason behind the Republic's transition into a monarchy, in this case the relativelymild' Augustan Principate. Individual leaders play a crucial role in shaping the events that transpired in Rome from the Gracchi to Augustus. However, neither the Gracchi nor any other prominent politician can be held solely accountable for the turmoil and revolution that befell the entire Roman political system (7 Deininger: Explaining the Change from Republic to Principle in Rome, published by BYU ScholarsArchive, 1980-84), since even the masses cannot always be "manipulated" at will. Therefore, any adequate explanation must include mass actions, attitudes, and loyalties, as well as their background. To continue with the previously mentioned explanations, attempts have also been made to attribute the fall of the Republic and the establishment of the monarchy to factors other than the deeds of "great" or influential people. These factors include significant modifications to the social and economic structure overall, most notably the massive growth of slavery during later Republican periods. It is impossible to explore the myriad variations on this fundamental notion, which is genuinely unique to the modern era—no author from antiquity assigned slavery this status—but which has become increasingly popular since the 19th century, possibly as a result of the abolitionist movement. It should be noted that Theodor Mommsen, a renowned scholar, gave slavery credit for being a major factor in the fall of the Roman Republic in his Roman History.

The explanation based on slavery has had its greatest success in the Soviet Union and other East European countries with Stalin's notorious doctrine of the "revolution of slaves" in antiquity. There it was even held that the end of the Republic and the rise of the Principate must, in principle, be explained by the reaction of slave owners (or rather,'slaveholders') against the imminent danger of a slave "revolution," as it had appeared during the great slave revolts in the late Republican period. "There were very old social weaknesses" (uralte soziale Schaden), he says, "by which the Roman commonwealth (das romische Gemeinwesen) perished."

Roman society, or more specifically, the propertied classes of Rome, were perceived as reacting to Spartacus' uprising by toppling the Republic and establishing the Principate. The addition of this extreme, one-volume Comparative Civilizations Review must be made immediately. Although mandatory for a while, the majority of East European ancient historians have long since given up on the one-sided and distorted view of late Republican Roman history presented in 4 [1980], No. 4, Art. 5 https://scholarsarchive.byu.edu/ccr/vol4/iss4/5. This one-sided and distorted vision is still maintained by some party philosophers and occasionally appears in secondary school textbooks. Naturally, these observations shouldn't overshadow the real contribution that the late Republic's growing slave population made to the notable decline of a sizable portion of the Roman populace, particularly the liberated Roman peasantry. However, it also seems that the slaves' role was merely incidental and was insufficient to account for Rome's political system's transition from republican to monarchical structures.

I believe that the traditional "theory of moral decline" belongs in the category of explanations that focus on less important or incidental elements of the transition from republicanism to monarchy. There is much that has been said and much that could be said about this, but I will confine myself to a few points here. As was previously mentioned, this theory was developed at a time when the outcome was still unknown, and for this reason, it should be considered a theory about the fall of the Republic rather than a theory explaining the transition to monarchy. Once more, there is no question that changes in attitudes, values, and morals among the upper classes preceded or coincided with political change, and that these changes played a significant role in what is commonly referred to as the "disintegration" of the major social groups in Rome in the final century B.C. Not to focus on other challenges here, but it is necessary to show that 'morals' and values were of a lower calibre during the imperial era than they were during the Republic in order to accept moral decline as an explanation for the fundamental shift from a republic to a monarchy.

Overall, the 'theory of moral decay' inevitably favours the early and "classic" Republican era over imperial times.9 Deininger: Explaining the Change from Republic to Principle in Rome, published by BYU ScholarsArchive, 1980, 86. In fact, the existence of this prejudice is evident in the writings of many contemporary writers as well as in some ancient ones, such as Tacitus, who were greatly influenced by the so-called "return" of republican institutions and thought that is so characteristic of modern European (and, starting from there, global) history. However, with the exception of Tacitus, the idea that Roman republican manners, morals, and values were fundamentally superior to those of the monarchical system cannot be proven, and as such, it cannot serve as the foundation for an explanation of the political events that led to the transition of Rome from a republic to a monarchy. And lastly, the fourth illustration of the explanation focuses on ancillary elements. Although it is more of an "anti-explanation," E.S. has maintained it with amazing vigour. Gruen in The Last Generation of the Roman Republic (1974), a recent, comprehensive, and academic work Its primary conclusions with regard to the current issue can be summed up as follows, in my opinion: the Civil War that started in 49 B.C. was the only factor that ultimately led to the fall of the Roman Republic. and its repercussions and aftermath up to Augustus. It doesn't seem that the Civil War itself was seen as merely one more development in a string of ongoing conflicts within the Roman political system. Conversely, it originated primarily from several incorrect choices made by prominent politicians in the final months prior to the start of the conflict.

The Roman republican system had up until this point operated, in a sense, flawlessly; there had been no actual crisis of the Republic during the period between Sulla's death and the start of the Civil War. The author claims that there was no "crisis" during "the last generation of the Roman Republic," to use the language of his title. It is clear that both chance and the political mistakes of great men are commonplace in history. It is necessary to acknowledge their 10 Comparative Civilizations Review, Vol. Recognising the significance of 4 [1980], No. 4, Art. 5 https://scholarsarchive.byu.edu/ccr/vol4/iss4/5 87 in the formation of significant political events may be beneficial for historians to be reminded of. Even Sir Ronald Syme has acknowledged that "the conviction that it all had to happen is indeed difficult to discard," but any historical determinism must be rejected in the special case of the late Roman Republic and the transition from Republic to Principate. As one looks at the long and continuous series of increasingly powerful "imperatores" from Marius to Augustus, one gets a very strong impression of an "inner necessity" (the expression is Eduard Meyer's) leading inexorably to the final monarchical solution. Thus there can be no doubt that warnings expressed by scholars so unlike each other as the German Alfred Heuss and the late Russian Sergei L. Uttchenko against all "mere mechanics of evolution" and against the "teleological" point of view are justified and must always be borne in mind.

Nevertheless, an interpretation which goes so far as to reduce the causes of the change from Republic to Monarchy in Rome more or less to chance combined with a few political errors of the leading men in 50 B.C. can hardly be accepted. The statement that there simply were no underlying causes at all in the great shift from the republican to the monarchical way of life, is hardly in accordance with the vast dimensions of the change, with its slowness, its length, its definiteness and its irreversibility. It may be doubted, as well, whether analysis of events between 79 and 49 B.C. can lead to any theory covering the entire period of change from Republic to Principate. There have been, by the way, very different judgments on the date when the fate of the Republic finally was sealed; thus, in sharp contrast to our author's opinion, Mommsen thought that it had already happened long before the Civil War.

But however that may be, certainly no one will doubt that by the time of Augustus, change had definitely taken place; and from then on, evolution visibly worked in favor of a growing consolidation of Monarchy, culminating, it can be said, in the so-called "Dominate" of Late Antiquity. The whole history of the Roman Empire demonstrated the expediency and the significance of a basic change that cannot be explained, to take a quotation from Gruen's book, chiefly in terms of "accident and irrationality, stubborness and miscalculation." Again, nobody would deny, I think, that all these elements also played their role, somewhere, in the political events that finally led to the establishment of the Principate. But behind the basic process, the breakdown of the Republic and the appearance of Monarchy, there were much more momentous and even overwhelming, constant pressures and necessities that will have to be discussed presently. Thus we cannot consent to the general views presented in the Last Generation of the Roman Republic, but we may hope that systematic discussion about the causes of the change in the Roman political system will be stimulated by it. So much for kinds of explanations where too much weight seems to be given to minor or secondary aspects.

To stress that point again, I want to make it clear that all these views hitherto considered are in one way or another important and should not be simply rejected; the only thing one has to keep in mind is that they cannot be central to any explanation of the change from Republic to Principate in Rome; that is to say, with the examples given here, that neither the work of the Gracchi, nor the growth of slave labor, nor moral decline nor, finally, accident and irrationality can form a sufficient basis for an explanation why in the course of the first century B.C. the Republican government of Rome gave way to Monarchy. But then—what must be regarded as crucial elements of the whole process, on which 'explanation' may reasonably be based? In the first place and as a decisive factor in the evolution towards the Principate has to be mentioned the increasingly independent role, the 'emancipation' in a sense, of generals and armies from Senate and popular assembly, or to use Latin terms, the ever growing division between 'imperator' and 'miles' on the one side, and of 'senatus' and 'populus' on the other. It may conveniently be remarked here that as 'senatus populusque' in Rome (or, for that matter, council and popular assembly anywhere in classical antiquity) formed the base of the Republican system, so military leader and army were the keystone of most of the large monarchies. In Rome, the widening division between 'imperator' and 'senatus' in the higher ranks of society correspond, in a way, to the division between 'miles' and 'populus' in the mass of the Roman citizenry, and it appears that the causes which eventually produced a rift that went through the whole community of Roman citizens, were also the decisive causes of the breakdown of the whole republican system and the victory of Monarchy. In a sense, of course, the shift from Republic to Monarchy is only one element, albeit an especially visible and spectacular one, of much more comprehensive changes in the Roman state and society.

But as to the causes of that particular change, I think, there should be widespread agreement among scholars on the primary importance of this growing split in the Roman citizenry, even if it does not by itself provide a 'explanation' of the origins of Monarchy in Rome. It must be added that the change described here rather summarily as a simple 'split' in the Roman political community was something much more complicated, if considered in detail. But in the present context it is not necessary to explain, e.g., the nature of what Anton v. Premerstein called "adherence to military leaders" (Heeresgefolgschaft), the basic process being fairly clear. From this, however, the third question immediately arises: what were the causes of this internal split? How did this fatal and ever widening rupture in the Roman 13 Deininger: Explaining the Change from Republic to Principle in Rome Published by BYU ScholarsArchive, 1980 90 state originate? The answer must be, of course, that many different causes contributed to its growth. But there are in fact two main complexes that have received special attention by modern research which can provisionally be characterized by catch phrases like "social issue" and "decline of the free peasantry" on the one hand, and "disintegration of the nobility" on the other.

The first complex refers principally to the large masses of Roman citizens, while the second concerns mainly the upper classes. In reality, no doubt, there is much interdependence between the two. It is not possible to analyze in detail the familiar problem of the actual dimensions of the decline of the free peasantry and the role played by the pressures of the long and distant wars, by the competition of slave labor, the growth of large estates, etc. But certainly the social decline of the traditional free peasantry was one of the main prerequisites for the appearance of professional armies strongly tied to their 'imperator'. As to the second main complex, sometimes called the "disintegration of the Roman nobility," it too, evidently, has to be explained by a large number of single factors, notably the many problems and negative consequences of Roman domination in the provinces and the effects of the extraordinary commands of the first century B.C. One may say that the first complex is more a problem of domestic policy or internal affairs, while the second refers chiefly to problems of "foreign" or "external" affairs. Naturally, however, there is a strong interdependence between the two, and certainly the internal, 'social' problems considerably weakened the political position of the traditional upper class and contributed to its disintegration, while, on the other hand, for example, the expectations and demands of the soldiers were reinforced by the apparent dissolution of the solidarity of the senatorial class. Of course, all these single elements have been carefully studied and analyzed by modern research and are 14 Comparative Civilizations Review, Vol. 4 [1980], No. 4, Art. 5 https://scholarsarchive.byu.edu/ccr/vol4/iss4/5 91 familiar topics in late Roman republican history. As to their respective parts in the transition from Republic to Principate, they are frequently—and, after all, justly—placed beside each other, though that may happen in a rather unreflective manner.

A problem arises, however, if one tries (as frequently happens) to ascribe any definite priority to one or the other of the two great complexes, in the sense of a "primacy" of foreign or domestic policy to use an expression frequently employed in German historiography. Authors who incline toward a priority of 'external' factors tend to emphasize the completely changed needs of the practice and maintenance of Roman domination in the vast Empire: from this, there arose the pressures bringing about the 'disintegration' of the governing class. The enormous growth of political and military objectives and of the opportunities and temptations offered by Empire, to which were added certain cultural influences from the Hellenistic world, were, according to this interpretation, the decisive causes of the disintegration of the nobility and the concomitant loss of authority of the Senate. One especially important factor in this view was the granting of the extraordinary imperia, which led to the rise of certain military commanders and, in the end, to Monarchy.

This view tends to stress the fundamental lack of political consciousness and independence of the great mass of citizens. Several names could be mentioned to illustrate this. So one book, probably hardly known in this country (and forgotten in Germany, too), the Roman History of Carl Neumann (published posthumously in 1881) has in its first volume a very long chapter entitled "The causes of the decline of the Republic" nearly exclusively built upon this approach. It may deserve a special mention here, because it is one of the surprisingly rare attempts to analyze and describe in detail the causes of the breakdown of the republican system in Rome instead of presenting just a detailed narrative with some general remarks on these causes. 15 Deininger: Explaining the Change from Republic to Principle in Rome Published by BYU ScholarsArchive, 1980 92 But besides Neumann, there could be mentioned also, for example, Eduard Meyer, Friedrich Miinzer and Matthias Gelzer—all outstanding experts in the field. One succinct sentence of Gelzer (in reviewing a book of Miinzer) may demonstrate at least one important variant of this interpretation: "He" (so Gelzer says of Miinzer) "in explaining the constitutional change places the main stress on the necessities of foreign policy. One need only remember the evolution of the notion of 'imperator' to realize the correctness of this view." Though it is not always presented in this rather strict fashion, this conception seems still to be strongly influential. On the other hand, priority might be given to 'inner' or 'social' causes, an interpretation that also has a long tradition. Mommsen's phrase pointing to the ruin of the middle class by slave labor as a 'last' cause of the downfall of the Republic has already been cited, although it must be added that his views are much more complex and, at the same time, may not be entirely consistent.

One could name other authors, too, who give a clear preponderance to social factors. I think that this is true, among others, of P. Brunt, or of Kurt von Fritz who has discussed at great length in his work on the mixed constitution in antiquity the causes of the change from Republic to Monarchy in Rome; besides, he emphasizes certain weaknesses of the Roman republican "constitution" as being responsible for the shift from

Republic to Monarchy (or rather, as he prefers to call it, to "cesarism"). A recent example of this general approach might be found in a German dissertation published a few years ago (1974). Its author, Helmut Schneider, has since written what might be called another, more popular, version of his views on late Roman republican politics, as well as several articles in defense of his interpretation. According to his view, the crucial causes for the end of the republican system were the erroneous economic policy of the Senate and its fundamental inability (or unwillingness) to satisfy what the author calls "the social interests of the socially outcast citizens." The "conflict between army and Senate" that brought about the decline and the end of the Republic is essentially, in his view, a conflict between a proletarianized peasantry and the owners of large estates. The author takes express exception to theories which emphasize "external" factors, and he states explicitly in contradiction to the views of Matthias Gelzer and Chr. Meier (while citing in support P. Brunt) that the causes of the decline of the Roman republic are not to be found at all in the growth of the Empire, in the expansion of political objectives or the widening gap between the institutions of the city-state and the worldwide Empire, but basically and exclusively in a social conflict between the landless and the owners of the "latifundia." It may be acknowledged, after all, as a merit of this author, that he has made explicit some controversies in modern views on the decline of the Republican system in Rome that frequently exist only in a rather implicit or hidden manner in current literature. Nevertheless, it must be clear that neither alternative offers a satisfactory solution or, to use again the German terminology already mentioned, that a "primacy of foreign policy" in an explanation of the constitutional change in Rome would be as questionable as a "primacy of internal affairs." Factors of 'foreign policy' such as the extraordinary commands or the needs of administration, as important as they may have been, are not sufficient to explain the transition from Republic to Monarchy. So it could easily be shown, for example, that the development of a central and provincial 'bureaucracy' began for all practical purposes only after the definite establishment of the Principate and then proceeded only slowly.

Against too strong an insistence upon the role of extraordinary commands it has rightly been objected that they remained, during the late Republican 17 Deininger: Explaining the Change from Republic to Principle in Rome Published by BYU ScholarsArchive, 1980 94 period, limited and restricted to exceptional cases. Moreover the final establishment of the Principate by Augustus (though it profited from existing forms of imperia extraordinaria) can least of all be explained by "necessities of foreign policy" (to repeat Gelzer's expression).

It may be noted, too, that the general passivity of the provincial populations (which has often and rightly been emphasized) also lessened the need of a strong and centralized executive power in the Empire. On the other hand, the one-sided interpretation of the shift from the Republic to Monarchy in terms of 'domestic policy' and 'social issues' alone is no less dubious. The characteristic view (as it is presented by the above-mentioned German author) of the Principate as a "military dictatorship" with, as compared to the Republican system, "greater efficiency in safeguarding the interests of the propertied classes in Italy and in suppression of social unrest," to quote him directly, certainly does not do justice to the reality of the Augustan or later Principate. In the Italy of the first century A.D. there was hardly any urgent need to suppress political or social unrest.

If the Principate has any claim to the "repression" of social classes, then, it was the suppression of internal strife among the elite itself, which also was the source of the only, rather weak opposition to the Principate during the first century A.D. At the same time, it is a misunderstanding to regard the domestic struggle between "army and Senate" or "expropriated peasantry and big landowners" as being responsible for the breakdown of the Republic. In this interpretation (which in addition omits all the important elements of foreign policy) really significant struggles among the power elite itself are wholly ignored and they, as it should be clear, cannot be explained exclusively in terms of 'social issue'. This approach too is one-sided, insofar as it tries to explain the crisis of the Republic and the rise of Monarchy only in terms of social conflicts. The one safe conclusion to be made is that it is not possible to give any specific priority to one of the two main complexes we have briefly discussed here.

The ultimate question appears to be, rather, in which way these two chief areas of conflict are related to each other or if they (so to speak) arose independently of each other and combined incidentally to create the rupture in the Roman republic, and thus to bring about the destruction of the Republic and give birth to the Monarchy. The answer certainly will be that these two different spheres of conflict and tension in the Roman Republic did not originate in isolation from each other, but that both, to summarize them briefly, the "social questions" as well as the "disintegration of the nobility", were the results of one comprehensive phenomenon, that is, the continuous, incessant growth of Roman domination, the manifold, decisive consequences of which affected the governing class no less than the mass of citizens. It may be said, and to put it briefly, that as political expansion could be accomplished only by all parts of Roman society, "senate" and "people," so the consequences of it affected both of them, although, as no one will be surprised to see, in wholly different ways. But it should be clearly recognized that the final political outcome, the enduring and permanent establishment of Monarchy in Rome, can in no way be separated from the enormous extension of territory, or, to put it in still other terms, that the 'irreversibility' of the whole process repeatedly emphasized here and so characteristic of this constitutional change in Rome, must be explained primarily by the unparalleled extension of the Roman territory— unparalleled, at least, by any republican state. So we have to return, finally, to the general thesis hinted at occasionally already in antiquity and stated very formally, for example, by

Montesquieu, according to which it was ultimately the prodigious territorial expansion of Roman domination which through many 19 Deininger: Explaining the Change from Republic to Principle in Rome Published by BYU ScholarsArchive, 1980 96 intermediate effects 'enforced', as it were, the transition from Republic to Monarchy, or, if you prefer a more reserved description, which was its decisive prerequisite. This also, to be sure, has been contested, the main argument against it apparently being that Roman political expansion had already by the third and second centuries B.C. reached dimensions far beyond the size of the classical, 'republican' city-states, without any visible imminent danger for the existing republican system of government.

The supporters of the thesis linking final constitutional change and the dimensions of Roman expansion and domination must, according to E.S. Gruen (and others), indicate one fixed point, one particular stage in Roman domination, a quantum, as it were, at which the republican system necessarily changed beyond hope of reversal. There will be little doubt, that, put in these terms, this argument serves mainly to suggest the absurdity of the 'expansion thesis'; for it is, of course, clear that political history (and history in general) is not obedient to simple 'quantum mechanics' of this kind. The connection between territorial expansion and the shift from Republic to Monarchy cannot however be cast aside in this way. It would be easy, indeed, to show that if the crisis finally became open only with the struggle about the agrarian reforms proposed by the elder Gracchus, there had already been clear signs of increasing difficulties in the system of

Republican government, paralleling the growth of Roman domination; the growth of domination was indeed accompanied by the slowly increasing effect of the factors already mentioned, which worked with such fatal effects upon the masses as well as upon these prominent in Roman society. Finally, our understanding of the change that took place in Rome might be enhanced by placing it in a wider perspective of ancient history, a perspective which frequently seems to be ignored by historians of Rome but which may further clarify what may be called the non-incidental nature of the whole process and its characteristic 'irreversibility.' So I hope you will permit me to make still some more general considerations about the relationship between the size and the governmental structure of a given territory as we see it in antiquity.

It seems, first of all, that in the whole of antiquity republican forms of government were chiefly restricted to quite small territorial units of government, or, as they are aptly called, "city-states." This must, of course, be stated here simply as a matter of fact; any attempt to explain it would lead us too far away from our present subject. One important additional feature of these ancient 'republican' city-states was the fundamental role played by primary, 'popular' assemblies as opposed to potential representative institutions. We must leave aside the vast problem of representative government in antiquity, which has been discussed notably by J.A.O. Larsen. But, in a sense, one cannot escape the conclusion that the very notion of political representation remained foreign to the citizen of classical times or, for that matter, to the ancient city-state; and one main reason for the importance of primary (as opposed to representative) assemblies in antiquity was, again, the characteristic smallness of the city-states. On the other hand, evolution did not stop at the city-state, and there did indeed arise republics or republican political units much larger than mere city-states: one may mention, for example, the 'Greek federal states' or sympolities; and there no doubt developed quite comprehensive political units at least led or dominated by republican, that is, non-monarchical governments—as, for example, the Delian League, the Carthaginian Empire, or, of course, the Roman Empire of the Republican epoch, by far the greatest of them all in territory and population.

But even here there evolved no recognizable system of representative government, and one principal cause for this must be sought—to state it briefly—in the fact that 21 Deininger: Explaining the Change from Republic to Principle in Rome Published by BYU ScholarsArchive, 1980 98 the governmental structure of these larger political associations always remained closely tied to their basic models, which were the institutions of the city-state. One could point for a further illustration of these remarks to the special case of Italy in the comparatively short period from the end of the Social War to the establishment of the Augustan Principate: the Appenine peninsula was doubtless the largest territory in all antiquity to possess, if only briefly, a consistent 'republican' organization. But obviously one must admit that with this unique example we are already in the midst of 'crisis'; and indeed one could demonstrate very well with this example, the problems arising from the absence of any system of representation. In many aspects, however, all these political units transcending the city-state, but with a certain kind, at least, of republican 'head', important as they may have been for the political history of the Mediterranean world, must be viewed rather as exceptions.

Monarchical, not republican government is the rule (one is tempted to say the 'law') in all large and what may be called territorial states of antiquity, in all ancient Empires. This holds true for all antiquity—and not only for classical antiquity, but starting from the ancient Oriental empires of the third and second millenium B.C., from the Assyrian and Persian empires to the monarchies of the Diadochs; it holds true no less, if I may add, for India and China, and I think one can even say that it holds true, roughly speaking, for 'pre-modern' times as a whole. In a sense, it can be maintained (as often has been done) that only since the late 18th century, that is, with the American and French revolutions, have Republican structures begun to appear in large territorial states. Thus this is a phenomenon characteristic only of modern times. Far away as all that is from the Roman republic, I think nevertheless that it may seem worthwhile to put the Roman republic for a moment in this wider perspective, because only then its uniqueness, 22 Comparative Civilizations Review, Vol. 4 [1980], No. 4, Art. 5 https://scholarsarchive.byu.edu/ccr/vol4/iss4/5 99 not only in antiquity, but in the whole of pre-modern history, becomes clear. It may be added that the limitation of republican government to small units (and especially to city-states) before modern times may be seen not only in the existing states of these epochs, but may also be seen as an influential part of political doctrine.

This doctrine was until modern times in perfect accord with political and historical experience, including as the most striking example Rome's transformation into Monarchy. The origins of the doctrine can be traced, I think, at least as far back as the 14th century, to the great Italian jurist Bartolus de Saxoferrato, in his Tractatus de regimine civitatis; and notwithstanding the objections made by David Hume and others mentioned in the beginning of this lecture it remained very influential until the 18th century. There are many interesting examples of its importance even after the American and French revolutions (notably in those European countries that upheld Monarchy through the early 20th century); but to list them will not be necessary here. It seems illuminating to me to place the Roman republic of the last century B.C. within these wider, if frequently ignored, historical perspectives, because only then does the extraordinary and quite exceptional position of the Roman republic of the first century B.C. begin to emerge, not only in classical antiquity or the ancient world but in pre-modern history as a whole.

The Republic that finally and irreversibly turned to Monarchy was an exceptional phenomenon because, as by far the greatest in size and population of all pre-modern republics, it was the most anomalous; thus, it may appear less strange that it 'failed' and was transformed into Monarchy, there being no tradition whatsoever of representative government. As to the links between the size of a unit of government, the problems of apparently limitless growth, and change in political structure, it may be argued that Rome, after all, is the only case where a transition from 23 Deininger: Explaining the Change from Republic to Principle in Rome Published by BYU ScholarsArchive, 1980 100 Republic to Monarchy can be observed in this manner. This is essentially true, although it would be possible to discover trends to monarchical government in other large 'republics' of antiquity. But there exists nevertheless one kind of historical 'check' which should not be overlooked and which can confirm to some extent the correspondence that existed between size and constitution. For example, some centuries earlier, in the world of Greek poleis, there had been very strong tendencies toward monarchical government, in the form of 'tyranny'.

But all the almost countless attempts to establish and to consolidate a kind of monarchical power within the city-state failed utterly, as is well known, in the long run. It seems certainly to be characteristic both of the extraordinary force and of the limited range of the republican system in the ancient Mediterranean, that tyranny, essentially a monarchical form of government, never grew into a lasting monarchical system within the narrow area of the city-state, while on the other hand Monarchy was not only established, albeit after a long critical period, in the vast Roman Empire, but gained continuously more strength as well as lasting and undisputed predominance.

Thus, it may be said that within the vast Roman Empire there occurred exactly the opposite of what had been the case in the innumerable small city-states of earlier classical antiquity. Viewed in this perspective the Roman "revolution" leading from the Republic to Monarchy appears, as it may be emphasized here, not as something really .new (which the contemporary notion of ' revolution", after all, tends to suggest) but rather as the disappearance of something new and unusual—the large Republic state—and its replacement by a quite venerable principle of government, that is, by Monarchy; and it could be asked whether a change of this kind should, from a wider perspective, properly be called a "revolution" at all. But if the shift to Monarchy appears from a modern point of view to be a movement 'backwards', leading, in a sense, to a more 'archaic' structure of government, it meant, for antiquity, a political structure much more efficient and stable, at least in very great territories. Nevertheless, as we have seen, the republican structure of government has never before modern times had a development comparable in size to that of Rome in the last century B.C. So what remains remarkable and astonishing and demands explanation is, in a sense, less the eventual transition from Republic to Monarchy or Principate, a step, as we may say, which merely 'normalized' the political pattern of so vast an empire, but, on the contrary, the extraordinary vigour and tenacity of the traditional republican order in Rome. There was ultimately no power that could prevent its breakdown or rather its transformation into Monarchy, as a lasting consequence of excessive political expansion. To a certain, if diminishing, extent even the Principate and the later Empire, as is well known, were still imbued with republican remnants; and so it may seem in a sense appropriate that, from the Roman 'libera' res publica there came to the large modern republics their very name, tied no longer, as during the classical epoch, basically to the city-state. UNIVERSITAT HAMBURG 25 Deininger: Explaining the Change from Republic to Principle in Rome Published by BYU ScholarsArchive, 1980.

2.12 The Parthian Empire's Formation and the Power-Transition Crisis of the 160s-130s BCE

The Hellenistic era began with Alexander the Great's conquests across the ancient Mediterranean and Middle East. During this time, the Seleucids, one of the most prosperous successor dynasties, dominated the majority of the Middle East. However, Parthia and Rome, two ancient powers on the rise, were instrumental in the Seleucids' eventual collapse. In a previous article, I contended that the Parthian state's establishment in Iran was partially caused by geopolitical developments in the Eastern Mediterranean during the middle of the third century BCE. The 240s and 230s saw a sharp fall in Seleucid power due to disastrous military conflicts both at home and abroad in the west, which is what political scientists refer to as a "power-transition crisis." This article argues that, following a period of recovery, a further abrupt decline in Seleucid power in the 160s-130s sparked another power-transition crisis that ultimately ended Seleucid hegemony over the Middle East. It does this by drawing on similar methodologies to historical analysis and international relations theory. The crisis made it easier for the Parthian state to quickly grow from a small kingdom to a powerful empire, fundamentally altering the ancient world's international landscape.

Alexander the Great's conquests in the Middle East were ruled by the Seleucid Empire at the beginning of the third century BCE. The Hellenistic era, which Alexander and his successors brought about, was marked by a strong Greek cultural and linguistic influence on the conquered eastern lands. The Levantine coast, Syria, northern Mesopotamia, and Armenia in the west, and the central Asian steppe and the Indus River valley in the east, roughly define the region that is sometimes referred to as the "Hellenistic Middle East." At the height of their power, the Seleucids ruled over these territories. One of the world's biggest and most culturally varied states was the Seleucid Empire. Its borders were wide, and its wealth was enormous. The empire's greatest drawback, however, was its enormous size and diversity. Such a vast and diverse empire could only be held together by the strongest of kings at the best of times. Sadly, for the Seleucids, such men were in short supply.

The Seleucid Empire endured a harsh existence, beset by constant dynastic unrest and savage conflicts with multiple rival Hellenistic states, chiefly Ptolemaic Egypt. However, Parthia and Rome, two ancient powers on the rise, were instrumental in the Seleucids' eventual collapse. Even though most academics still believe that the Romans were mostly to blame for the "irreversible weakening of the Seleukid Kingdom," the Parthians, also called the

Arsacids, were ultimately the ones who irreversibly weakened Seleucid authority.

The Parni, a nomadic tribe that eventually came to be known as the Parthians, were first settled in what is now western Turkmenistan in the early third century. The Parni had been travelling south and west for decades in search of a safe and prosperous place to call home (Just. Epit. 41.1.10-11). Eventually, a geopolitical crisis throughout the Hellenistic Middle East, where the Seleucid Empire fractured under the pressures of civil war, rebellion, and invasion, facilitated the Parni's conquest of northeastern Iran. Once in power, the victorious Parni quickly persuaded the Parthian aristocracy in the region to support them against the interests of the Seleucid state and its officials. Ultimately, they tried for several more decades to gain access to the well-positioned, wealthy lands of the Iranian plateau in order to gain protection from violent neighbours, increased state security, political opportunity, and the ability to establish and cultivate a strong powerbase.

The Parthian state's founding sparked a significant rivalry between the Seleucids and Parthians that lasted for 1.5 centuries and culminated in the Parthian conquest of the majority of the former Seleucid Empire. According to Roman historian Justin (Epit. 41.1-3), the Parthians were a strong and resilient people who had survived their lowly beginnings, outlasted many better-positioned rivals, and emerged as Rome's final rivals.

The Parthians were no longer content to share power within the Hellenistic Middle East, and they suddenly and with great energy began to invade and occupy neighbouring regions at the direct expense of the Seleucids. The Parthians, for the first time, established an empire that became the most threatening rival of the Seleucids in the Hellenistic Middle East. Under Mithridates I and his immediate successors, the Parthian kingdom transformed into what international relations theorists call an "unlimited revisionist state." These Parthians were not content to share power within the Hellenistic Middle East, and they became determined to dominate the entire region.

2.13 IR Theory and Parthia's Ascent

The Parthian state was a sophisticated and extremely successful imperial power that rivalled the capacities and achievements of any ancient state, despite the fact that it was undoubtedly very different from the contemporary nation-states that gave rise to international relations theory. The growth and development of the Parthian state, which scholars usually discuss in the traditional terms of political history—good leadership, the inclusiveness of Parthian rule, Parthian adaptability, or the declining strength of Parthia's neighbours—is better understood with international relations theory, specifically the theoretical framework of ealism. Realism emphasises the unforgiving and competitive nature of interactions between states within an international system of states that lacks enforceable international law and/or central authority, known as interstate anarchy. This article employs Realist Theory (specifically a Neorealist or "structural" approach to international relations, which is the study of how system structures affect international behaviours and outcomes) as a framework to help provide greater perspective and a more expansive understanding of state decision-making and interaction in the ancient world. In this endeavour, I share Eckstein's preference for the use of the sub-school of realist theory called "offensive" realism when analysing ancient international environments because of the comparatively primitive and violent characteristics of these environments in the ancient world. Offensive Realism maintains that states seek to maximise their security and power through domination and hegemony because of the anarchic nature of many interstate systems (or international communities in which states interact and compete). Systems of militarised interstate anarchy were common in the ancient world, including the systems that developed in the Hellenistic Middle East.

Seleucid dominance over their eastern territories abruptly decreased in the 240s and 230s as a result of several expensive battles with Ptolemaic Egypt and internal dynastic strife. In particular, the sudden death of Antiochus II (in 246), the Seleucid defeat in the Third Syrian War (246-241), and the subsequent civil war for the throne (ca. 240-236) severely damaged the reputation and military might of the Seleucid Empire. This unexpected decline of Seleucid power in the 240s caused what international relations theorists call a "power-transition crisis" (or a sudden and dramatic fluctuation of a state's power within an interstate system) in the Hellenistic Middle East. Although a power-transition crisis does not in and of itself cause war, it makes hegemonic war, which is a large-scale war that reorders or creates a new interstate structure that better reflects the realities of power distribution and balance of power within the system, more likely because it destabilises the interstate system and brings power relations into question. This is precisely what happened in the 240s-230s as Parthia and Bactria emerged as rival powers to the Seleucid Empire on the Iranian plateau.

With the emergence of rival states within the Hellenistic Middle East in the middle of the third century, the international environment once dominated by the Seleucid Empire suddenly and drastically changed. Parthia in northeastern Iran and Bactria in Afghanistan challenged Seleucid hegemony on the Iranian plateau, and the major interstate system, which had incorporated all the Greek lands of the eastern Mediterranean and the Persian-held regions of the Middle East since the Persian Wars, abruptly and effectively split. What International Relations theorists call an interstate system of "tripolarity" (or the rivalry of three dominant states) between Antigonid Macedon, Ptolemaic Egypt, and the Seleucid powerbase in Syria remained in place in the west in the new, more focused "Eastern Mediterranean interstate system." Yet a turbulent and rather ambiguous tripolarity between Parthia, Bactria, and the Seleucid Empire also emerged in the east in what we may call the newly formed "Iranian interstate system."

Parthia and Bactria were no longer directly concerned with the geopolitical developments and rivalries of the eastern Mediterranean after the Iranian interstate system emerged in the 230s. Furthermore, the geopolitical developments of the Iranian interstate system were only sporadically and indirectly related to those of the eastern Mediterranean interstate system through sporadic Seleucid efforts to reclaim their lost eastern lands in the 230 s, 200 s, 180 s, 160 s, 130 s, and 120 s.

Since all of our surviving sources see events in Syria and Babylonia as distinct from one another during this time, the Seleucid Empire thus came to operate simultaneously in separate major interstate systems—a geopolitical distinction shared by several other large, powerful empires throughout history. Additionally, the geopolitical developments in the east, particularly those pertaining to Parthia, had no direct connection to the emerging international environment of the Graeco-Roman Mediterranean world. Rather, they belonged to an independent interstate system in the east that was only marginally impacted by events in the west.

The political, cultural, and economic emphasis of the Seleucids distinguished their involvement in the Iranian interstate system from that of the eastern Mediterranean interstate system. As the Persians and Alexander's imperial heirs in the Middle East, the Seleucids established one of the greatest empires in history during this time. But they seem to have approached their hegemony in the east with a slightly different perspective than their forebears. Alexander and the Persians had viewed their imperial space as limitless on the central Asia steppe and in the Indian subcontinent; however, Kosmin recently argued that the Seleucids formed stricter limitations on their imperial space, especially along their eastern frontier, with "explicit and formal recognition of equal peer kingdoms."

Although, at least in theory, it is unlikely that the Seleucid kings abandoned their royal ideology of unlimited, universal rule, practical concerns in the west encouraged the Seleucids to develop a more restricted policy in the east. Therefore, Kosmin's arguments for the limitation of Seleucid hegemony in the east, where the Seleucids actually restricted and shrank the limits of their imperialism when they created an "ideological limes" along the frontier of the central Asian steppe and in 306/305 ceded the Indus River valley and Arachosia (modern southern Pakistan) to the Mauryan Emperor, Chandragupta, in exchange for 500 war elephants, generally appear sound. The Seleucids decided to establish Bactria (modern northern Afghanistan) as a bulwark to protect the eastern edge of their empire and turned their attention to the geopolitical developments of the eastern Mediterranean.

The Seleucids were active, aggressive, and frequent participants in the eastern Mediterranean interstate system because they came to value western geopolitical developments and rivalries. However, the Parthians and Bactrians continuously exploited the Seleucids' western distractions to maximise their regional security and power, escalating their own regional rivalry. In the meantime, their participation in the Iranian interstate system was reactive, inconsistent, and sporadic. The Seleucid state remained an important power in the east, possessing the potential strength to threaten the survival of Parthia and Bactria.

The recently established interstate systems in Iran were similar to those in the Mediterranean. It was an unforgiving global setting full of bellicose, aggressive, and militarised polities. Beyond open conflict, there was no way to comprehend the reality of power relations between states, no enforceable international law, and no means of ameliorative diplomacy. Hellenistic kings, indigenous Iranian dynasties, and tribes in central Asia posed a serious threat to the Parthians' security and survival. Although the Seleucid state was weakened and the Seleucid kings were diverted by the crisis of the 240s–230s, which broke the eastern frontier, the Seleucid state's potential power remained significant. Five different Seleucid kings—Seleucus II, Antiochus III, Antiochus IV, Demetrius II, and Antiochus VII—would attempt six campaigns to reconquer the eastern lands over the course of a century, a testament to their unwavering resolve to oppose the Parthians and reclaim their lost territories. However, only one of those efforts proved to be effective. The Parthians battled to both survive and eventually grow within the Iranian interstate system, and their policies were influenced by this unstable and dangerous international environment.

In the late third and early second centuries, the Parthians survived through bloodshed and compromise, trying to survive in a hostile and dangerous environment where mass enslavement, massacres, and even total destruction were constant concerns. However, by the middle of the second century, another major crisis engulfed the Hellenistic Middle East, providing an opportunity to maximize their security and power. Within a generation, there was another abrupt and significant shift in the global environment. As the Seleucids' real adversaries, the

Parthians took control of many of the lands previously occupied by Alexander's successors, profoundly influencing the development of eastern history.

2.14 The Breakdown Occurs

Arsaces I, the first Parthian king, established a powerful independent state in northeastern Iran by the 230s. When Seleucus II, the son of Seleucus I, invaded to retake these lost lands, the Parthians defeated him, solidifying their position and preserving the Parthian kingdom. Seleucus III, Seleucus' son, then took on the task of reestablishing Seleucid hegemony over the Iranian plateau. During a massive campaign (210-205), Antiochus III, Seleucus II's son, conducted a grand campaign (210-205), reoccupying large portions of eastern Iran, western Afghanistan, and southern Pakistan. He also established Parthia, Bactria, and an Indian kingdom in the northern Indus River valley as subordinate allies (Polyb. 10.28.5-31.1-13, 11.34.9-12; Just. Epit. 41.5.7). Regretfully, Antiochus' eastern campaign had compelled the kings of Parthia and Bactria to become his subordinate allies; however, the instability of his new network of subordinate allied kingdoms posed a significant challenge to the succeeding Seleucid kings. The previous arrangement had to be renewed diplomatically or through force once Antiochus or one of his subordinate allies died. Few of Antiochus' successors possessed the same level of military prowess or diplomatic influence, and the Parthians' skill and tenacity were crucial in undermining the viability of Antiochus' loose imperialism model over subordinate allied kingdoms in the east in the second century. Since the Seleucid king's competence in many ways dictated the ability of the state to maintain its hegemony, the Seleucid Empire failed, particularly in the east. A fresh eastern campaign was therefore required roughly once every generation to preserve or restore Seleucid hegemony in the east because there was little incentive to submit to the Seleucids once new leaders appeared in Parthia and Bactria.

Furthermore, the outcome of Antiochus III's war against Rome (1924-188) fundamentally altered the global landscape once more. The Seleucids operated within three major interstate systems: the Mediterranean interstate system, which was dominated by the Romans; the Iranian interstate system, which was dominated by the Seleucids; and the developing multipolar Near Eastern interstate system, which extended from Egypt to eastern Anatolia, the Caucasus, and Mesopotamia. Along with the actions of many middling and minor states, such as the Hasmonean Kingdom in Judaea, Cappadocia in southeast Anatolia, Pontus in northeastern Anatolia, Armenia, and various Arab tribes, this new Near Eastern interstate system featured the rivalry of the Seleucids and Ptolemies.

Even though the Seleucid Empire continued to rule the Iranian interstate system in the 180s-170s, the Parthians took advantage of many opportunities to regain and strengthen their former strength due to a series of military and political setbacks and distractions in the west. [41] By the 160s, however, the Seleucids to the west of Parthia and the Bactrians to the east of Parthia faced growing difficulties that contributed to the creation of another power-transition crisis in the Hellenistic Middle East. This time, the Parthians—particularly under Mithridates I—

came out to be the main winners of this crisis. The Seleucids obviously understood how crucial it was to maintain their unwavering hegemony across the Iranian plateau. Actually, Antiochus III passed away in 187 while getting ready for a second eastern campaign. [Antiochus IV, Antiochus' youngest son, then set out on an unsuccessful eastern expedition in early 165.

The Parthians' abrupt and brutal invasion of Hyrcania (modern-day northern Iran) in early 165 distracted Antiochus IV from his task of quelling the Maccabean Revolt in Judaea. The Maccabees' fifth book (7.10-13) documents,

And the deeds of Mattathias and his son Judas were reported to King Antiochus [IV]. The king of the Parthians, or the king of the Persians, was also informed of this; consequently, he [probably Phraates I] betrayed Antiochus by breaking off their friendship, imitating Judas. "I have now determined to go into the land of Persia [that is, Parthia] to make war; and I wish to leave behind my son [Antiochus V] in my stead; and to take with me half of my army, and to leave the remainder with my son," Antiochus said, calling one of his household officers, Lysias, a stout and brave man, to him. This gave Antiochus a great deal of uneasiness.

These accounts show that late in his reign, Antiochus left Judaea hurriedly to pursue a war against the Parthians in the east. Tacitus (Hist. 5.8) states, "King Antiochus [IV] endeavoured to abolish Jewish superstition and to introduce Greek civilization; the war with the Parthians, however, prevented his improving this base of peoples; for it was exactly at that time that Arsaces had revolted [desciverat]." Scholars, starting with Moore, have accused Tacitus of not knowing that Arsaces I seized Parthia in the middle of the third century and of confusing Arsaces I's actions here with the Maccabean Revolt. However, the precise context of Antiochus' eastern campaign is disputed, and some scholars reject Tacitus' comment as an error because of his use of the name "Arsaces." Nonetheless, there is good reason to reject such criticisms. Tacitus' comment does not establish a definitive link between this "Arsaces" and Arsaces I. In fact, the Romans were aware that all Parthian kings, regardless of their given name, adopted the name Arsaces as a royal title upon their ascent, just as the Romans did with the titles Caesar and Augustus. It is much more likely that Tacitus here is simply referring to the Parthian king who is currently in power by his regal name, Arsaces. Consequently, we need to take into account, first, who the Parthian king was in 165 and, second, what this man had done to capture Antiochus IV's attention (Just. Epit. 41.5.1-6; Strabo 15.1.36).

The conventional timeline places Mithridates I's accession to the Parthian throne around 171, which would indicate that Antiochus IV launched his eastern campaign to thwart Mithridates' escalating ambitions in the east; nevertheless, there is conflicting evidence that Mithridates assumed the throne in 171. Rather, Assar has recently presented a strong case for moving the start of Mithridates' reign forward to ca. 165/164 and to modify the reign of Phraates I to ca. 168-165/164. As a result, Phraates, Mithridates' elder brother, might have held the throne when Antiochus launched his eastern campaign. Actually, this new chronology is supported by additional evidence found in the passages from Tacitus and V Maccabees. Tacitus says the Parthians had "revolted," and in V Maccabees, the Parthian king betrayed Antiochus' "friendship." These descriptions make much more sense if we associate them with phages instead of mithridates.

The V Maccabees passage may suggest that after Antiochus III's death, Arsaces II, Phriapatius, Arsaces IV, and Phraates I, among others, reestablished their friendship with Seleucus IV and Antiochus IV. However, it is evident that the Parthians did not behave kindly towards the Seleucids for a long time, as evidenced by Phraates I's attack on the Mardians and subsequent reoccupation of Hyrcania in early 165 (Just. Epit. 41.5.9). Phraates may have even intentionally taken advantage of the Seleucids' overburdened logistical burden by attacking Hyrcania during the time they were occupied in Judaea.

Thus, Phraates drastically altered the relationship between the Parthians and Seleucids, not Mithridates I, finally breaking off amicable relations and violently rebelling against Seleucid hegemony. Phraates I's sudden western expansion was a blatant violation of the status quo between the Parthians and Seleucids established by Antiochus III. Antiochus IV was alarmed by Phraates' sudden aggressiveness and success, and a swift Seleucid response was required. Antiochus launched a massive retaliatory campaign with half of the Seleucid military with the intention of punishing the Parthians and regaining Seleucid hegemony over the east.

I passed away around Phraates. 165/164 He designated Mithridates I, his younger brother, as his heir. Phraates set aside a number of his adult sons in order to accomplish this (Just. Epit. 41.5.9-10). Phraates' decision to leave the kingdom in his brother's more capable hands to maintain the positive momentum of the dynasty and state may have been motivated by his fear of his rapidly deteriorating health. Mithridates, too, shared his brother's emphasis on an assertive foreign policy, and Phraates' decision proved crucial as Mithridates built on his brother's momentum to elevate the Parthian state to unprecedented heights of power.

According to international relations theory, during the lengthy reign of Mithridates I (ca. 165/164-132), the Parthian state underwent a transformation from a limited revisionist state that sought to maximise its security in the region to an unlimited revisionist state that sought to supplant the Seleucids as the dominant power in the Hellenistic Middle East. The Parthians were no longer content with regional power and influence on the Iranian plateau; instead, they were determined to replace them with their own hegemony. Mithridates' capable and aggressive leadership was central to this transition.

Anabasis (210-205) of Antiochus III had decimated the Parthian kingdom. The Parthians were warned about the potential threat of neighbours and the need to maximise state power by the aggression of the Seleucid state, the Parthian military's failures, and the sharp turn in Parthian fortunes at the end of the third century. Justin claims that the Parthians came to exact revenge for the Seleucid state's aggression (Epit. 42.1.1). In addition to regaining the lost territory of Arsaces I's kingdom, Mithridates I sought to position Parthia as the dominant force within the Iranian interstate system. Opportunity, motivation, and capability all lined up for the Parthians as Mithridates used hegemonic war to settle old scores against the Seleucid Empire. This was a momentous time in Parthian history that merits more thought and consideration. Like his brother, Mithridates was a fearless and talented military commander who did not lose any time in completing the reconquest of Hyrcania by taking advantage of the Parthian military's increased strength.

Antiochus IV prepared his eastern campaign in 165, closely imitating his father Antiochus III, after realising that the Parthians' resurgent aggression posed a serious threat. Initially, he gathered a sizable army, appointed reliable administrators to oversee his territories in the west, and safeguarded the standing of his youthful son, Antiochus V (App. Syr. 8.45; V Macc. 7.10-13; cf. I Macc. 3.27-37). Second, by conquering Armenia, he established his northern border (Diod. Sic. 31.17a; App. Syr. 8.45, 11.66; Porph. 38, 55-56). In the end, he looked for a substantial quantity of money to finance his journey to the east.

Antiochus IV also made the decision to attempt to plunder a temple in southwestern Iran, possibly as retaliation for his father's violent death, and needed money to finance his own major eastern expedition (Polyb. 31.9; Joseph. AJ 12.354-9; App. Syr. 11.66; II Macc. 9.1-3; Porph. 56). Antiochus III had attempted to loot a temple in southwestern Iran in 187, but he had died in the attempt. . His attack encountered a similar level of firm opposition and was utterly unsuccessful. Unlike his father, Antiochus survived the attack; however, his expedition to the east was derailed by his failure in southwestern Iran. He no longer had the men or the money to launch an instant attack on the Parthians. Antiochus unexpectedly passed away in late 164, probably from illness, near Gabae (modern-day Isfahan, Iran), although the exact cause is hotly contested in the sources.

Antiochus IV of the East suddenly died, leaving the Seleucid throne in the hands of his nine-year-old son, Antiochus V. During his brief reign (1641-1661), there was a great deal of political intrigue, conflict, and Roman influence (App. Syr. 8.46-47; Joseph. AJ 12.360-361). Lysias, the boy's regent, was too preoccupied with issues in the west to investigate Antiochus IV's plans to subjugate the Parthians. Because of this, the rapidly expanding Parthian state was spared a significant invasion that would have seriously threatened its recently regained independence. Mithridates I was also able to continue his aggressive foreign policy and military operations across the Iranian plateau during this period of Seleucid retaliation. Following Antiochus IV's untimely death, the Seleucid government fell, perfectly conforming to the theory of the "power-transition crisis," in which one interstate system pillar abruptly loses strength while another gains it.

The power-transition crisis of the 160s-130s, like the one that followed Antiochus II's setbacks, gave the Parthians a tremendous opportunity to sharply increase their power and stature at the direct expense of the shattered and disoriented Seleucid Empire. Additionally, like the Seleucid governors Andragoras in Parthia and Diodotus in Bactria during the 240s-230s power-transition crisis, the 160s-130s power-transition crisis gave satraps in Media (northwestern Iran), Elymais (southwestern Iran), Persis (southern Iran), and Characene (southern Mesopotamia) the chance to rebel. Mithridates I and his government established Parthia as the dominant force on the Iranian plateau and the main adversary of the Seleucids in the developing Iranian interstate system, as the Seleucid Empire started to fall apart once more.

THE CRISIS IS STILL THERE.

Following his accession to the throne in 175, Antiochus IV named his close friend Timarchus viceroy of the Upper Satrapies (App. Syr. 8.45; Diod. Sic. 31.27a). Timarchus was the principal figurehead responsible for preserving the power and sway of the Seleucids in the east, while Antiochus battled the Ptolemies and Jews in the west. Timarchus observed Phraates I's sudden aggression from his headquarters in Media, where he attacked the Mardian army and started to retake Hyrcania. As a matter of fact, Timarchus was probably the official who alerted Antiochus in Judaea to the gravity of the Parthian threat (V Macc. 7.10-13). Timarchus was one of Antiochus' most trusted allies and influential advisors, so his warning would have been taken seriously. This explains why Antiochus reacted so quickly to the worsening circumstances in the east. Antiochus appears to have included Media in his plans for attacking the Parthians and is likely to have communicated with Timarchus during the campaign, even though it is likely that he marched his army from Judaea through Syria, Armenia, Babylonia, Elymais, and finally to Persis in southern Iran before his unexpected death. However, Antiochus' untimely death in 164 abruptly ended his plans of eastern conquest, left the Parthians unaffected, and isolated Timarchus.

Antiochus V, the boy king, was unable to hold onto his position or rule the kingdom after Antiochus IV passed away. The twenty-two-year-old cousin of Antiochus V, Demetrius, and his father's advisors Lysias, Philip, Timarchus, and Heracleides fought for influence and power within the waning empire. Like Andragoras and Diodotus before him, Timarchus quickly made the decision to declare independence in Media due to the lack of a powerful central government to aid in defending the empire's eastern regions and the growing threats to his lands' security. The Seleucid state was in danger of collapsing due to yet another round of civil wars.

According to international relations theory, the Hellenistic Middle East experienced another power-transition crisis as a result of Parthia's unexpected aggression and the unrest that followed Antiochus IV's death. The Parthians were able to expand the boundaries of the Iranian interstate system and cause it to overlap with the lands of the Near Eastern interstate system for the first time thanks to this crisis, which lasted from the late 160s to the early 130s. A dangerous international environment of heightened uncertainty and anxiety between polities had been fostered by the rapidly changing geopolitical situation in the Hellenistic Middle East by the late 160s. For instance, Justin (Epit. 41.6.1-3, 6-7) highlights the violence of the international environment and the uncertainty of power relations between Parthia and Bactria during this period, emphasising Bactria's sudden and unexpected decline under the pressure of "various wars" and Parthia's rise "to the highest degree of power."

The Parthians' unexpected return to power in the Iranian interstate system fundamentally changed the balance of power. The Seleucid hegemony temporarily broke down into a multipolar system of multiple competing polities during the power-transition crisis of the 160s–130s, which was facilitated and prolonged by widespread conflict and rapid change. The interstate anarchy within the Iranian interstate system, which included factors like increased militarism, a lack of security, and fear of destruction, encouraged aggression and open conflict between multiple states and statesmen during the crisis to eliminate potential threats and establish a new, more reliable distribution of power throughout the Hellenistic Middle East. The hostile and unstable international environment of the Hellenistic Middle East during the power-transition crisis of the 160s–130s assisted in encouraging

Mithridates I had a fantastic chance to establish an assertive foreign policy and grow his kingdom at the expense of the Parthians' adversaries because of this unstable environment. Mithridates' first objective was Bactria's strategic frontier region. The Bactrian kings' attention was gradually diverted from their unstable borders to the north and west by ongoing dynastic conflicts and an ongoing rivalry with the Indo-Greek Kingdom in northern India. In this unpredictable atmosphere, Bactria became more susceptible to Parthian and nomadic aggression during the crisis.

By the middle of the 150s (and possibly as early as 163/162), Mithridates I had successfully fought a war against Bactria. The Parthians gained control of the western parts of Aria (western Afghanistan) and Margiana (eastern Turkmenistan) during this conflict, greatly expanding their eastern territory and elevating their stature within the Hellenistic Middle East. Mithridates even used new imperial imagery on his coinage to symbolise his victory over the Bactrian Greeks. His victory significantly shifted the balance of power on the Iranian plateau in Parthia's favour, and Bactria never again emerged as a major player in the geopolitics of this region.

After more than ten years in media, solidifying his wealth and power, Timarchus found himself in a precarious situation when Antiochus IV unexpectedly passed away. Timarchus was unable to exert any influence over Antiochus IV's young son, Antiochus V, who was in the hands of the royal advisor Lysias in Syria. Timarchus was unable to stop his cousin Demetrius I from taking the Seleucid throne after he escaped from captivity at Rome in 162-161, killed Antiochus V and Lysias, and proclaimed himself king in Media shortly after. Timarchus quickly raised "an army of considerable size" and formed a military alliance against Demetrius with King Artaxias of Armenia, who had used the crisis to reassert his independence (Diod. Sic. 31.27a).

Timarchus quickly extended his domain outside of the media by using his sizable army and newfound coalition. Although Diodorus exaggerates Timarchus's victory in the war against Demetrius I, Timarchus started to refer to himself as the "Great King" and may have taken control of

Media Atropatene and Elymais before occupying Babylonia in 161/160. Diodorus (31.27a) states, "Having, moreover, intimidated the neighbouring peoples by an impressive display of force and brought many of them under his sway, he marched against Zeugma [on the Euphrates] and eventually gained control of the kingdom."

The actions of the Parthians during the Seleucid civil war remain a topic of debate among scholars. The Parthians were eventually prompted by the crisis to invade Media; however, it is unclear if Mithridates I attacked Media prior to Timarchus marching west to fight Demetrius I. Olbrycht recently argued that Timarchus likely repelled Parthian attacks in the late 160s, allowing him to secure his eastern frontier before invading Babylonia. Meanwhile, Grainger suggests that Timarchus and Mithridates made an agreement that limited Parthian expansion westward. Lastly, Taylor asserts that Timarchus "scored a major victory over the Parthians and used this victory to proclaim himself king." Despite this, there is simply no evidence that directly connects Timarchus to a conflict or a treaty with the Parthians.

Timarchus and the Parthians are linked by scholars to a passage in Justin (Epit. 41.6.6-7) that reads, "A war arose between the Parthians and Medes during the course of these proceedings among the Bactrians [that is, the Indian wars of Eucratides, and after fortune on each side had been some time fluctuating, victory at length fell to the Parthians." With this newfound authority, Mithridates appointed Bagasis over Media while he marched into Hyrcania. Justin shows that there was a protracted struggle for media, but he also makes it clear that Eucratides' invasion of India came about after Mithridates' successful campaign against the Bactrians in the late 160s or early 150s. In addition, Timarchus' reign was brief after his invasion of Babylonia in 161. With Demetrius I's conquest of Media and Babylonia shortly following Timarchus' defeat in 160, there is very little chance of a confrontation between Timarchus and the Parthians.

Taylor's claim that Timarchus soundly defeated the Parthians and crowned himself king is not supported by the evidence. Diodorus, in fact (31.27a), clearly shows that Timarchus proclaimed himself king in direct opposition to Demetrius I's usurpation. Meanwhile, Grainger's conclusion that Timarchus would not have been able to rebel in Media if the Parthians had been free to attack him ignores the fact that Androgoras and Diodotus had exactly that in the face of the Parni's aggression under Arsaces I in the 240s. Timarchus' rebellion was actually caused by the breakdown of Seleucid authority following Antiochus IV's death and the increasing influence of Mithridates I. Furthermore, there isn't much evidence to support Grainger's theory that Mithridates and Timarchus forged a treaty.

Timarchus had been Antiochus IV's stalwart ally, threatening to subjugate and punish the Parthians in 164. However, Timarchus was inspired to proclaim his own kingship by Demetrius I's usurpation of Antiochus V's throne, which led to a civil war. Although Timarchus harboured animosity towards the Parthians, he was unable to launch an assault on Parthia in 162-161 prior to addressing Demetrius in the west. In the meantime, Mithridates I had little incentive to voluntarily restrain his own western military ambitions or to make friends with the antagonistic Timarchus (Just. Epit. 41.6.6-9). It was only conceivable that Timarchus and Mithridates would reach a beneficial treaty following a decisive battle, of which there is no proof.

It is improbable that Timarchus and the Parthians engaged in combat in the latter part of the sixteenth century, despite the beliefs of many modern scholars. Before invading Babylonia in 161/160, Timarchus would have needed time to gather his army, form an alliance with Armenia, and establish his dominance over his immediate neighbours, had he proclaimed himself king in 162/161. Even after Antiochus IV's death, Timarchus had spent more than ten years fortifying Media's defences, and Mithridates I was well aware of the significant influence he held there. Timarchus's conscientious efforts, of course, also contributed to the reason why it took the Parthians so long to conquer the area. Timarchus was one of the most powerful men in the Hellenistic Middle East in the late 160s, according to Diodorus (31.27a), and he used his position of strength to intimidate and compel his rivals in the region. Actually, Timarchus probably scared off some of the surrounding peoples early in his reign with his impressive show of force, including the Parthians.

The Parthians were still a minor force in the late 160s, only now starting to make a comeback after decades of decline. Mithridates prepared for the defence of Hyrcania and Parthia in 165/164 after consolidating his brother's recent territorial gains. Antiochus IV's failed eastern campaign prevented an invasion of Parthia, but Timarchus' position in Media remained strong.

Timarchus was encouraged to exercise caution in media by Mithridates' lack of resources in 163-162 and the unravelling crisis within the Seleucid Empire.

Timarchus and Mithridates were at a loss for words. Without first obtaining additional resources, neither leader could possibly hope to overpower the other, so they focused on other objectives. Mithridates soon focused on the precarious frontier of Bactria after Timarchus became embroiled in the Seleucid civil war in the west. Before Timarchus took control of Babylonia in 161 and died in 160, Mithridates had not had time to plan and carry out significant operations against Media after winning his war against Eucratides I and seizing control of large areas of Aria and Margiana. Therefore, it is likely that Mithridates' protracted and challenging campaign to subjugate the media did not begin until the 150s.

2.15 The Median Conquest by the Parthians

The Hellenistic Middle East fell into the power-transition crisis of the 160s-130s, which increased the likelihood of a large-scale conflict between the Parthians and Seleucids even though Timarchus and Mithridates I did not go to war in the late 160s. The eastern regions of the Seleucid Empire grew more susceptible to the Parthians' growing power, and the Parthians' renewed aggression on the Iranian plateau forced Seleucid retaliation. Conflict had already arisen in Media, Babylonia, Aria, and Margiana, and rebellions in Elymais and Persis further destabilised the region. During this time, the Parthians progressively attempted to usurp Seleucid hegemony and take control of the Hellenistic Middle East, which led to the beginning of a new phase of hegemonic warfare between them and the Seleucids that would determine the new balance of power in the Iranian interstate system.

By the end of the 160s, the Parthians had gained control over Aria, Parthia, Hyrcania, and Margiana, which greatly enhanced their financial and logistical resources. Mithridates I was better positioned to take on the Seleucids in the west because he had more resources and a more formidable eastern frontier. The Parthians found significant political and financial benefits from Western expansion into Media, Persia, and Mesopotamia; nevertheless, the Seleucids and local dynasties repeatedly posed a threat to Parthia's growing hegemony, making the conquest and occupation of these areas exceedingly challenging.

The empire's integrity was briefly restored when Demetrius I took back control of Media and Babylonia following Timarchus' defeat in 160. Because of Demetrius's victory in this civil war, Grainger recently proposed that Mithridates I waited ten years to attack media following Timarchus' defeat because "the Seleukid state under Demetrios I was strong enough to deter any adventure by the Parthian King." Nevertheless, this argument oversimplifies Demetrius' position in the 150s and is too dismissive of the evidence. Even though Demetrius defeated Timarchus, he was preoccupied with matters in the West, and his hold on the empire was tenuous.

After his release from captivity, Demetrius I had strained relations with the Romans, which he did not improve even after taking control of Syria (App. Syr. 8.45-47; Polyb. 31.11-15; I Macc. 7.1). When Demetrius tried to intervene in Cappadocia (southeastern Anatolia) in 159, the Romans swiftly overruled his decision. Justin (Epit. 35.1.1) states, "Demetrius, having possessed himself of the throne of Syria and thinking that peace might be dangerous in the unsettled state of his affairs, resolved to enlarge the borders of his kingdom and increase his power by making war upon his neighbors." Justin illustrates that Demetrius realised his precarious position, and it is not surprising that he chose to act aggressively to expand his The Romans' decision to defend Cappadocia was intended to reassert their hegemony at the direct expense of Demetrius' regime, and the situation in Cappadocia was an embarrassment for Demetrius that called into question his strength and legitimacy, severely limiting his effectiveness in the 150s. Nevertheless, Demetrius was unable to invade Cappadocia or to install a puppet ruler because of the severe limitations of his power and influence within the Roman-dominated Mediterranean interstate system.

Alexander Balas publicly challenged Demetrius for the Seleucid throne in 152 as a result of Antioch's rebellion against his rule following the Cappadocian disaster. Despite Alexander's feeble claim to the throne, Demetrius persisted in mishandling his affairs, and Alexander eventually won the support of the Jews and Ptolemaic Egypt in the civil war (I Macc. 10.1, 21, 46-47, 51-58; App. Syr. 11.67). In 150, Demetrius lost his life fighting Alexander after failing to replicate his victory over

Timarchus (Just. Epit. 35.1.9-2.2; I Macc. 10.48-50; Joseph. AJ 13.116-119).

Demetrius I thus devoted his entire turbulent reign (162-150) to quelling uprisings, battling for the throne, and attempting to reassert the empire's dominance. He was not capable of acting with the ferocity with which he would have liked to act against Parthia and other neighbouring states. According to Justin, the conquest of media by Mithridates I was a protracted process marked by several setbacks. Moses of Chorene reports that Mithridates engaged in combat with Demetrius' generals in Media during this struggle. Demetrius was never powerful enough to "deter" the Parthians from attacking the media. Actually, his weakness and inefficiency made the Parthians more inclined to attack his lonesome generals in the east.

There is simply insufficient evidence to support Grainger's recent conclusions, which state that Mithridates I did not attack Media until after Alexander Balas became king in 150 in order to avoid Demetrius I's power, that Mithridates justified his attack against Alexander because he was a Seleucid usurper, and that Mithridates hoped to restore Achaemenid legitimacy under the Arsacid dynasty. Rather than using strong ideological or propagandistic justifications to justify his aggression against the Seleucids in Media, Mithridates began his campaign to conquer Media and Media Atropatene as early as 158 and no later than 155. Mithridates had far more compelling practical concerns, such as expanding his power against a vulnerable rival, and Demetrius' regime was vulnerable. The Arsacids were not yet concerned with the dynastic politics of the Seleucids, and the Parthians' interest in an Achaemenid revival for their imperial propaganda arguably did not develop until their much later conflict with imperial Rome.

Demetrius I was compelled to focus on the empire's western affairs during the crisis, but despite this, the Parthians encountered slow and challenging conquest in Media due to resolute resistance from several Seleucid generals, which was partly enabled by Timarchus's earlier efforts to establish the area as a military stronghold. Mithridates likely subjugated Media Atropatene as a tributary kingdom in the north; however, the strong defensive positions of the Seleucids in the south and their successful counterattacks turned the campaign into a war of attrition. An unfinished Greek-Aramaic inscription on a carving of Heracles Triumphant at the Bisitun Pass in what is western Iran today, dated 148, gives us a good indication of the back-and-forth Seleucid and Parthian contest during the long conquest of Media. The inscription asks for the safety of Cleomenes, the Seleucid viceroy of the Upper Satrapies in Media at the time. The association of the inscription with Heracles Triumphant perhaps indicates that Cleomenes had won a victory against the Parthians as late as 148, signifying one of the many reversals of the Parthians' fortunes during this conflict mentioned by Justin. The inscription also illustrates that the Seleucids still occupied parts of Media in 148 and that the permanent Parthian conquest of the region was not complete until after this date. Mithridates marked his final annexation of Media by making his brother the new satrap of the region in ca. 147, in addition to releasing a run of commemorative coins.

THE PROBLEM GETS WORSE.

The Hellenistic Middle East's power-transition crisis of the 160s-130s was sustained by the Parthians' persistent aggression and a string of Seleucid civil wars. Demetrius I was also weak and subject to western concerns, even though Alexander Balas killed him in battle in 150 (Just. Epit. 35.1.9-2.2; I Macc. 10.48-50; Joseph. AJ 13.116-119). (I Macc. 10.51-8; Diod. Sic. 32.9c) Alexander had been a usurper of dubious lineage, and his attempts to obtain legitimacy through a marriage alliance with Ptolemaic Egypt had finally failed. Furthermore, in 147, as Media finally fell to the Parthians, Demetrius' eldest son, Demetrius II, arrived in Syria with the backing of Ptolemy VI to challenge Alexander's throne, and the Seleucid Empire once more descended into civil war. His generals in the east continued to thwart Mithridates I's advances in Media, but they were unable to completely eliminate the Parthian threat to the eastern lands of the empire.

Alexander Balas was soundly defeated in battle by Demetrius II and Ptolemy VI in 145, and they managed to have him assassinated. Despite Demetrius's victory, Media was lost, and he was forced to cede control of Coele Syria to Ptolemaic Egypt in return for Ptolemy's military backing and a marriage to his daughter, Cleopatra Thea. Furthermore, Demetrius' regime was beset by dynastic strife, incompetent administration, and weak military leadership. Demetrius soon discovered that the Seleucid state's growing factionalism presented him with a number of potential rivals as well as a number of disgruntled communities. The general Diodotus Tryphon was prompted by the general unrest in Syria to run for the position of guardian of Antiochus VI, Alexander's young son, and the Seleucid Empire entered an even more protracted and challenging civil war from 145 to 138.

The Seleucids' prestige, power, and influence were all at stake during this crisis, and to make matters worse, their concerns extended beyond Rome, Ptolemaic Egypt, and Parthia. Elymais and Persis in southern Iran seem to have followed the lead of Parthia, Bactria, and Media in the 160s, declaring their local autonomy and momentarily seceding from the Seleucid Empire. Later, in the 140s, the growing unrest within the Seleucid state made it possible for Elymais and Persis to reclaim their independence. At the same time, Characene, which ruled the Euphrates and Tigris deltas, also actively started claiming its autonomy during this time (around 141). Furthermore, the Seleucid state's vulnerability made it easier for Arab raids to start infiltrating the southern frontier.

However, the Parthians had materialised as the most immediate danger to the Seleucid state's existence. The Parthians eagerly stepped in to fill the power vacuum left by the collapse of Seleucid hegemony and the sharp rise in conflict throughout the Hellenistic Middle East during the crisis. Even though it was challenging, Mithridates I's conquest of Media and his authority over the Zagros Mountain passes were essential to the Parthians' subsequent westward and southward advance. Furthermore, commanding media gave the Parthians direct access to the vital breeding grounds of the renowned Medesan horses. [109] The Parthian military needed a growing supply of high-quality horses, and while there is no proof that the Parthians specifically targeted this area to obtain this resource, commanding these breeding grounds would have bolstered their army. Media soon rose to prominence as a hub of Parthian wealth and power, and as the crisis worsened, Mithridates started to target the affluent, urbanised, and exposed regions of Mesopotamia in the late 140s.

2.16 The Challenging Western Frontier of the Parthians

Regretfully, the accounts we have for this part of Mithridates' reign are hazy and frequently contradict one another. After completing his conquest of Media, Mithridates returned to Hyrcania, according to Justin (Epit. 41.6.7-8). He would later go back to the west to conquer Elymais and Mesopotamia. However, according to a piece of the Babylonian Astronomical Diaries, Mithridates took control of Babylonia by the summer of 141, went back to Hyrcania, and marched on Elymais.

By late 147, the Parthians had successfully conquered and occupied Media, but it would take several more years to establish Parthian rule over the area. Mithridates had to keep a close eye on events in the east as he and his brother Bagasis set about the difficult task of fortifying Parthia's new western frontier (Just. Epit. 41.6.6-7). In 145, Mithridates probably made his way back to the east in reaction to two fresh dangers. First, and more importantly, the kingdom of Bactria was beginning to fall apart under the mounting pressures of the invasions of the nomadic

Saka and Yuezhi. In particular, the wealthy and prosperous northern city of Ai Khanoum likely fell to these invaders in ca. 145. First, the Bactrian king Eucratides I died in 145 at the hands of his son. As a result, Mithridates needed to return east to ensure that the new king of Bactria—Helicocles I, Eucratides II, and Platon—had no plans to act a 146/145. Bactria had always been a crucial defence against the tribal confederations in this area, but as a result of dynastic conflicts and wars in India, the Bactrians lost strength and the Yuezhi were violently displaced, which led to a period of widespread migration for both the Saka and the Bactrians towards Sogdiana (modern-day southern Kazakhstan, eastern Uzbekistan, Kyrgyzstan, and Tajikistan). Eucratides I was dead, and his kingdom was rapidly collapsing, so Mithridates could not ignore the increasing vulnerability of Parthia's eastern frontier. Mithridates had tripled the area of the Parthian state since taking over as king in 165/164, elevating Parthia to the top of the Iranian plateau, but the Parthian hegemony in the east was still in jeopardy. While in the east, between 147 and 141, Mithridates presumably subdued tribes in southwestern Pakistan and Iran, as well as consolidating and fortifying the Parthian state's expanded borders.

At least for a while, Mithridates I's persistent attempts to fortify and guard his eastern frontier were effective; nevertheless, the rich regions of Mesopotamia, Elymais, and Persis continued to be alluring targets along the vast western frontier of the Parthians. In order to attack the core of the Seleucid Empire, Mithridates made the decision in 141 to jeopardise the security of his eastern frontier. Late in the spring, Mithridates invaded and conquered Babylonia, which the Seleucids had largely abandoned during the civil war that was still raging in Syria between Demetrius II and Diodotus Tryphon. Appointing governors of Macedonian descent, Mithridates entered the historically significant cities of Seleucia and Babylon as a victorious conqueror, maximising support in the area.

At this point, Persis most likely came under Parthian rule. Mithridates may have planned to gather his forces in Media, possibly close to Ecbatana, and then launch a swift, two-pronged attack. He undoubtedly led the main Parthian force that overran Babylonia, but Persis seemed to be subdued by a reliable general—possibly Bagasis. The Seleucids continued to challenge Parthian hegemony in Mesopotamia for decades, but these lands were now firmly established within the bounds of the expanding Iranian interstate system. Also, these conquests marked another important step in the rapid growth of Parthia as an unlimited revisionist state within that interstate system. The vast lands of Mesopotamia had been a part of the separate Near Eastern interstate system since the 180s. This created what international relations theorists call "system overlap" between the separate Iranian and Near Eastern interstate systems.

Mithridates, I launched his most forceful and direct campaign in 141 to challenge the Seleucid Empire's waning hegemony in the Hellenistic Middle East. One obvious symbol of the Parthians' newfound dominance was their hold on Seleucus I, the royal capital. In actuality, Parthia was much more than just a regional power because of its control over Media, Persis, and Babylonia; in particular, the Parthians gained enormous wealth and prestige from their occupation of Babylonia's great cities. Mithridates promptly issued a new series of silver tetradrachms (S13.1-2) in Seleucia on the Tigris to celebrate his victory and placate the region's sizable Greek and Macedonian populations.

For the first time, the Parthians could legitimately assert themselves as the hegemonic rivals of the Seleucids after taking control of Babylonia and Persis, which served as the Achaemenids' administrative centres, Alexander the Great, and Seleucus I. Moreover, Mithridates had a great chance to turn Parthia from a small kingdom into an imperial power during the power-transition crisis of the 160s-130s. More confrontation between the two powers was guaranteed by the Parthians' success and the threat they posed to the Seleucids. The Parthians, who continued to expand westward for another fifty years, had no intention of limiting their western ambitions to this region as the emerging hegemon in the Iranian interstate system and as a newly formed unlimited revisionist state. The Seleucids could not allow the Parthian aggression, and in particular, the loss of Babylonia, to go unanswered.

The security of the Seleucids and Parthians was threatened by a number of other issues during this time, despite the imminent possibility of another major conflict between the two dominant powers of the Hellenistic Middle East. Mithridates I once again made an abrupt return to the east after the conquest of Babylonia in 141, according to the Babylonian Astronomical Diaries. Mithridates' quick return to the Iranian plateau serves as evidence that, first, the conquests of Babylonia and Persis in 141 had been opportunistic and aggressive, and second, the eastern frontier remained vulnerable. Even though we lack concrete proof of military conflicts between the Parthians and the Saka during this period, Assar—using a passage from Strabo—suggests that Mithridates returned to the east at this time to counter steppe invaders. Mithridates recognised the serious threat posed by the encroaching nomadic warriors and thought his eastern lands were vulnerable.

The fact that Mithridates I chose to go back to the east further demonstrates his lack of understanding of the Parthians' immediate obstacles to their conquest of Babylonia. The recently independent Elymais people from southwest Iran invaded and started ravaging the area almost immediately after Mithridates left the region, according to the Babylonian Astronomical Diaries. The Elymaeans even set fire to Apamea on the Tigris before Mithridates and his generals launched a counterattack towards Susa, their capital.

Mesopotamia was thrown into chaos by the power-transition crisis of the 160s-130s, a period in which eleven different rulers held power in the region (Demetrius I in 160, Alexander Balas ca. 150, Demetrius II ca. 145, the Parthians in 141, the Elymaeans in 141/140, the Parthians in 140; Demetrius II in 139/138, the Parthians in 138, the Elymaeans in 138/137, and the Parthians in 137). [130] During this time, the region experienced destabilisation and destruction, which created opportunities and incentives for more violence. The

Parthians carried out forceful conquests after realising how unstable Babylonia and the surrounding areas were.

Justin documents that Mithridates I vanquished the Elymaeans and took control of Elymais, despite his jumbled chronology of events. However, the Parthians' conquest of Elymais was also highly intricate. In addition, even though Mithridates took Susa and produced a series of bronze coins (S12.26-28) from its mint in 140-138, it is possible that Diodotus Tryphon, the Seleucid usurper, attempted in vain to restore Seleucid control over Babylonia in 140. Shayegan has recently shown that Elymais and Parthia had an ongoing conflict over Mesopotamia and Susiana until the Parthians eventually forced Elymais to recognise Parthian suzerainty in 132 and accept Parthian direct rule in 124.

Before the battle with Parthia, Elymais had operated separately from the Seleucid Empire for a number of years. The Elymais rulers had declared themselves kings in 147 as a result of the devastating civil war between Demetrius II and Alexander Balas, and they proceeded to raid Babylonia for the next fifteen years. As a result, Elymais was one of many states in the growing Iranian interstate system that exploited the Seleucid hegemony's decline during the power-transition crisis of the 160s-130s, pursuing policies of power-maximising in order to boost state security and authority. Elymais, like Bactria, Parthia, and Media before them, chafed under Seleucid suzerainty in the first half of the second century, as did Persis, Media Atropatene, Characene, and Armenia, as well as other middling and minor states in the Hellenistic Middle East. These states wanted to govern themselves independently, but they were unable to withstand Seleucid reprisals until the abrupt decline in Seleucid authority that started in the late 160s and continued into the 130s.

The international environment was further destabilised by these middling and minor states' aggressive efforts to secure their own power and safety during the crisis, as well as their brief independence. Minor states had to be extremely belligerent and militarised in order to survive in an unforgiving system of interstate anarchy like the Iranian interstate system in the 160s–130s, where brutality and violence were constant threats. For this reason, it is not surprising that smaller powers, like the Hasmonean Kingdom, Commagene, Cappadocia, Armenia, Elymais, Characene, Persis, Media Atropatene, Bactria, the Indo-Greek Kingdom, various Arab and central Asian tribes, and especially Parthia, emphasised aggressive militarism against neighbouring powers during this time of crisis. The breakup of Seleucid hegemony in the middle of the second century meant that the Seleucids and Parthians had to deal with several highly militarised, expansionistic middling powers in addition to one another.

THE CRISIS'S AFTER EFFECTS

In this unstable and perilous global setting, the Seleucids resolved to exact revenge in the hegemonic conflict with Parthia. The Seleucid state continued to be a powerful military force in the Hellenistic Middle East despite recent civil wars, uprisings, and territorial losses to the Parthians, which severely damaged the authority of the Seleucid kings and the perceived power of the empire. Demetrius II and his successor, Antiochus VII, decided to launch significant eastern campaigns to exact revenge on the Parthians, salvage the Seleucid state's declining prestige, and restore the empire to its former glory. The Parthians had annexed Media, Persis, and Babylonia; however, each of these recent victories had been challenging, and none had involved the Seleucid royal army as a whole. The recent Elymaean raids into Babylonia demonstrated the precarious nature of the Parthian occupation of this area. The Parthians had to fight for years to conquer Media against the small forces of the Seleucids. In 140, Parthia's recently gained dominance in the east was still quite shaky. A determined and skillfully carried out eastern campaign, akin to that of Antiochus III in 210, could have quickly undone the Parthians' recent gains and restored Seleucid hegemony over the Iranian interstate system, if only momentarily.

Demetrius II and Antiochus VII had the chance, means, and will to launch significant eastern expeditions against the Parthians in 138 and 130. However, both campaigns ended in disaster as the Parthians' mobile and cunning warfare style isolated them and their armies. With these resounding wins, the Parthians cemented their position as the Seleucids' geopolitical equals and hegemonic rivals in the Hellenistic Middle East. The Parthians' victory gave them the opportunity to extend their lead into the Near East for the first time. Antiochus VII's eastern campaign was the last great gasp of the Seleucid Empire.

In the end, for three primary reasons, Mithridates I's Parthia emerged from the crisis as the most prosperous of many rival polities. First, the Parthians' relatively moderate and inclusive style of government aided them in their efforts to absorb huge swaths of territory throughout the Iranian plateau and Mesopotamia. The Parthians embraced regional aristocracies and incorporated them into a more flexible structure of empire. The Parthian state, from its conception, built upon the social flexibility of a multi-cultural union of regional leaders under the ultimate authority of the Arsacids. This made the high command of the Parthian state versatile and eclectic, allowing the Arsacids to develop a more inclusive system of administration that emphasised, utilised, and internalised the capabilities and strengths of local leaders. Although the Achaemenids utilised administrative inclusiveness and cultural flexibility to gain and maintain support within their massive empire, the Seleucids failed to persuade sufficiently "indigenous elites to identify imperial interests with their own." The more dismissive and exploitative occupation of the multi-cultural eastern territories by the Seleucids, which in the examples of Seleucus II, Antiochus III, Antiochus IV, and Antiochus VII resulted in disaster, created local resentment on a scale that the Parthians rarely encountered. Thus, compared to the Seleucid occupation of the Middle East, indigenous aristocrats had heightened regional autonomy and power under the Parthians, with greater access to authority and participation within the Parthian imperial system.

Second, the Parthians dominated the Hellenistic Middle East due to the makeup of their military, how they used it in the field, and their capacity to uphold a sizable imperial state. In order to outmanoeuvre and overpower their rivals, the Parthians employed a combination of swift, light-armed horse archers and possibly the most devastating and adaptable heavy cavalry in history during this time. Because their professional standing army was relatively small, they made use of their network of vassal kingdoms to raise the necessary levies and share the military burden of controlling such a large imperial territory. The Parthians developed a highly effective strategy to

Ultimately, the Parthian state's prosperity during this time was closely linked to the Arsacids' generally sound governance and relative stability. The Parthians had another significant advantage in their fight to rule the Hellenistic Middle East because of the stability of the monarchy during their early history, unlike the Seleucids and Bactrians, who were crippled by dynastic strife during the crisis. The Arsacids did not experience a civil war until the late 90s BCE. The state thrived under competent and strong Parthian kings such as Mithridates I, but when the king was feeble or the throne was in doubt, which happened far too often after the late nineties, the state's authority declined. However, the capable and ambitious early Arsacids were essential to the formation and expansion of the Parthian state from a minor kingdom to a major empire. The Parthian aristocracy's growing power was a major factor in the protracted cycle of civil wars that weakened the Arsacids starting in the first century.

As a result, Mithridates I's leadership was undoubtedly essential to the Parthian state's prosperity in the 160s-130s, and his numerous conquests made him one of Parthia's greatest kings. However, it's also vital to take into account the context in which he operated. The rapid collapse of Bactria and the death of Antiochus IV in the

160s and 130s created a power-transition crisis that made Mithridates' success all the more difficult, if not impossible. Antiochus's demise prevented a significant invasion of Parthia; multiple detours hindering Eucratides's government in Bactria allowed for easy eastern expansion; and Syria's crippling civil wars left Media and Mesopotamia vulnerable to invasion. It's important to comprehend Mithridates' reign's circumstances in order to fully appreciate his accomplishments. He wasn't the only leader who wanted to increase and solidify his position of authority, but he had tremendous potential and considerable skills.

Mithridates I took advantage of the greatest chance the Parthians had had to significantly increase their power and influence since the 240s-230s by positioning myself at the head of an ascending power during a time of widespread crisis in the 160s-130s. The Parthians skillfully and eagerly filled the power vacuum that the crisis caused throughout much of the Hellenistic Middle East, significantly altering the nature of the international environment. As Justin (Epit. 41.1.6-9) notes in his Parthian history introduction,

To all of them, it must seem amazing that the Parthians could rise to such a position of prosperity as to govern over the countries they had only been slaves to. Being attacked by the Romans in three wars, led by the greatest generals, and during the height of the republic's prosperity, they alone among all nations were not only a match for them but emerged victorious; though it may have been a greater glory to them to have been able to rise amidst the Assyrian, Median, and Persian empires, so celebrated of old, and the most powerful dominion of Bactria, peopled with a thousand cities, than to have been victorious in war against a people [the Romans] that came from a distance; particularly during the ongoing tense conflicts with the Scythians and other surrounding nations, as well as other daunting conflicts.

Here, Justin refers to the Parthians as the heirs and equals of the greatest eastern empires, highlighting the Parthians' continuous military victories and praising the importance of their ascent to power. The Parthians' rapid rise in the second century cemented their place in history as one of the greatest powers in the world, despite the fact that their rivalry with the Seleucids lasted for another fifty years and, shortly after, their rivalry with the Romans lasted for an additional three centuries.

Chapter Three

Power Transition; a Case Study of Vladimir Putin and Xi Jinping

A Comparative Analysis Of Vladimir Putin And Xi Jinping From A Christian Perspective On The Need For Change In Government Leadership

Leaders in politics frequently stay in their roles for protracted periods of time, if not forever. From a Christian perspective, this practice calls into question the significance of changing the leadership in the government. We will investigate this by concentrating on two significant figures, Xi Jinping of China and Vladimir Putin of Russia, whose prolonged administrations have attracted international attention. We will examine the Christian perspective on the need for regular changes in government leadership, including Christian-based principles, the role of leaders in Christian education, and the effects of long-term leadership on a country and its citizens.

3.1 Christian Principles and Values

A person's perspective on governance can be influenced by the values and principles that form the basis of Christianity. Among the essential ideas are:

Lowliness

One of the main virtues of Christianity is humility. It encourages people to act modestly and accept their limitations. From a Christian perspective, long-term leadership can lead to complacency and conceit. Leaders who hold long-term positions of authority run the risk of forgetting what the people's needs and concerns are. Lack of humility can result in power abuses and a disdain for the wellbeing of the populace.

Responsibility

Another fundamental tenet of Christianity is accountability. The Bible frequently holds leaders responsible for their deeds and choices. For example, leaders are compared to shepherds in the book of Ezekiel, who are in charge of their flocks. They will face judgement if they do not fulfil their duty. According to this theory, leaders should answer to the people they represent, and they should have the ability to change their style of leadership so that their actions can be assessed and improved.

Guardianship

Christianity places a strong emphasis on stewardship, viewing people as caretakers of the assets and obligations that God has entrusted to them. Leaders in the political sphere are custodians of the resources and welfare of the country. It is possible to view a change in leadership as a means of guaranteeing that new people will have the chance to properly oversee and manage the country's resources.

Fairness and Emotion

Fairness and compassion are highly valued in the Christian tradition, especially for the weak and disadvantaged members of society. Leaders who hold positions of authority for extended periods run the risk of losing touch with the problems faced by the average person. A change in leadership brings new insights and a revitalised commitment to resolving social injustices and providing for the underprivileged.

3.2 The Pastoral Function in Christian Education

Christianity also has teachings on the functions and characteristics of leaders. Instead of ruling the people, leaders are urged to serve them in the New Testament. In his epistle to the Romans, the apostle Paul emphasises how crucial it is to submit to ruling powers (Romans 13:1-7). It's crucial to remember, though, that respect for authority is dependent on leaders maintaining the rule of law and the welfare of the populace. The Christian view is that when leaders stray from these ideals, they ought to be held responsible and, if needed, replaced.

The Servant Leader

As demonstrated by Jesus in the New Testament, the idea of servant leadership holds that those in positions of authority ought to be modest, kind, and intent on meeting the needs of others. Long-term leadership can move away from servant leadership and towards self-serving leadership, particularly when accountability is lacking. A shift in leadership may usher in new people who are more dedicated to serving their constituents.

Fairness and Integrity

According to Christian doctrine, leaders ought to be agents of justice and righteousness. The significance of virtuous governance and the detrimental effects of unjust leadership are emphasized in the Book of Proverbs (Proverbs 14:34). Long-term leadership can cause moral decline and immoral behavior, both of which are bad for the country. A shift in leadership may present a chance to bring justice and righteousness back.

3.3 The Consequences of Extended Leadership

The leaders of Russia and China, respectively, Vladimir Putin and Xi Jinping, have held their positions of authority for protracted periods of time. By looking at their rule through a Christian lens, we can draw attention to some possible consequences of long-term rule.

Deterioration of Democratic Mechanisms

The possible erosion of democratic processes is one of the concerns from a Christian perspective. With its checks and balances that forbid the abuse of power, democracy enables the peaceful transition of power. Prolonged leadership has the potential to erode democratic norms that guarantee public accountability and representation.

Power Concentration

Long-term leadership frequently results in the consolidation of power among a small number of people. From a Christian perspective, this concentration of power may be problematic because it may result in abuses of power and a lack of accountability. The Bible stresses the need for humility and moderation as well as the perils of having too much power.

Repression of Opposition

Prolonged periods of power can lead to the suppression of dissent and opposition, thereby curtailing the freedom of speech and expression. This is troubling in a Christian context because it can result in the silence of voices that call for justice, morality, and the welfare of the populace.

Absence of Novel Approaches

governance may stagnate if current leadership is maintained without making any changes. In order to effectively address changing needs and challenges, new leaders often bring with them new perspectives and ideas. Christianity promotes flexibility and the search for solutions that advance society as a whole.

Putin and Russia's Vladimir

For more than 20 years, Vladimir Putin has held the dual roles of Russian President and Prime Minister, solidifying his position of authority. From a Christian point of view, there are various issues with his leadership:

Insufficient Accountability

Putin's leadership lacks accountability, which is one of the main issues. Christian ideas of accountability and stewardship are at odds with unchecked power, which can result from a lack of checks and balance

Repression of Opposition

Numerous incidents repressing political dissent and opposition have occurred under Putin's leadership, including restrictions on press freedom and the imprisonment of political opponents. The Christian values of justice, compassion, and accountability are challenged by this silence.

Power Concentration

Russia now has a concentrated government under Putin's long-term rule, leaving little space for other leaders. This concentration of power raises questions about potential abuse and a lack of humility from a Christian perspective.

Dubious moral and ethical behavior

If true, the claims of corruption and unethical behavior made against Putin during his presidency would raise moral questions for Christians. Christian values would place a higher priority on morality and righteousness in leadership.

3.4 Religion, State and 'Sovereign Democracy' In Putin's Russia

Church leaders have not prioritized the promotion of democratic governance because they were skeptical of liberal individualist visions of public life, committed to their role as the hegemonic religious institution, played a minimal part in the end of communism, and had little prior experience working within a democracy. In addition, there have been additional incentives for church and state to collaborate more closely in the wake of the 2011-12 political crisis, thanks to the political structures established by the Kremlin that promote a certain level of conformity and support for the regime among important social actors. In an indirect way, the church provides political support to the state; in return, the church sees a more vulnerable state as ready to advance at least some of its socially conservative agenda. Neither of them is particularly concerned with democratic governance in this situation.

However, in some historical contexts, religious attitudes towards democracy have veered in different directions. For example, the Roman Catholic movement changed from being broadly anti-democratic in the century and a half following the French Revolution to a position of critical support for democracy since 1945. Nevertheless, there is no compelling evidence to suggest that some traditions are inherently less democratic than others. In this piece, we concentrate on Eastern Orthodoxy as a specific religious tradition in the Russian Federation following 1991.

The Russian Orthodox Church had no prior experience living in a democratic society when it entered the post-communist era, having played a minimal role in the fall of the Soviet Union. In recent times, it has gained recognition as a crucial supporter of President Putin and has taken actions that might have strengthened the belief held by some that Orthodoxy is inimical to democracy. After communism fell, Russia began a transition whose end goal was commonly believed to be liberal-democratic but which actually developed in a different direction. Some academics focus on the essential components of democracy. Mikael Wiggel argues that these components must include both electoral (popular government) and constitutional (limited government) elements. He also lays out a number of requirements that a government must satisfy in order to be classified as a political democracy.

Although he focuses primarily on Latin America, it could be argued that Russia does not meet nearly any of his suggested criteria and cannot, therefore, be classified as a liberal democracy, much less a political democracy (Wigell 2008: 230-50). Some analysts would characterize the current political structures as "hybrid," combining aspects of democracy and authoritarianism, or they would emphasise that regimes exist on a spectrum, with Russia moving towards more overt authoritarianism following the 2011-12 elections (Hale 20110: 33-41; Petrov, Lipman, & Hale 2014: 1-26).

The Kremlin would dismiss the criticisms and contend that what has been established is a "sovereign democracy" that adheres to Russian traditional values. 1 However, this concept is rarely given much thought and is frequently defined by what it is not: a slavish copy of Western democracy. The rulers of this evolving module, which can be found in various forms in nations ranging from China to Iran, assert that the sovereign people give them authority, but as John Keane suggests, the people are both "ubiquitous and absent" (Ahmad, 2015: 85). In this way, what's emerging is a drastically reduced form of Schumpeterian democracy, in which "the people," subject to certain restrictions, are allowed to choose representatives to important positions; however, following elections, they are expected to remain silent or act as a chorus of support while the self-selected governed carry out their duties. It's unclear how religion fits into this political development.

The often-violent forced secularization that was encouraged by the Soviet Union has an impact on the society in which the Russian Orthodox Church functions. It operates in a society where two-thirds of people identify as Orthodox but where religious participation rates are similar to those in Northern Europe. Russia is still a secular state according to the 1993 constitution, which forbids the union of church and state, but in practice, there is less of a divide between the two. Politically speaking, it is not secular in that President Putin has forged a coalition of support with the socially conservative Russian Orthodox Church in recent years.

Its function in this regard is best characterised as that of a dominant church, since the majority of its members formally identify as Orthodox, its symbols and historical connections unmistakably link it to the Russian state's past, and it enjoys various forms of official recognition from state authorities. It says it doesn't want an establishment, even though it most likely has more political clout than the traditional Church of England. However, because the state does not grant it "exclusive legal, economic, or political rights denied to other religions," it does not fit the definition of a "hegemonic religion" as given by Jocelyne Cesari (Cesari 2014: 9). It may have hegemonic aspirations, but as we'll see, it also acknowledges that it is more than just primus inter pares. The idea that a true secular state does not ban religion from public life and, more importantly, that church and state collaborate for the benefit of the country is fundamental to this.

At first, President Putin expressed caution about this comprehension and emphasised that church and state were distinct in Russia during the discussions surrounding the introduction of religious education in schools between 2005 and 2008 (Anderson 2015: 169). But in more recent times, he has tended to emphasize—paraphrasing Samuel Huntington—that Russia's civilizational identity is fundamentally shaped by Orthodoxy. This political shift is based, in part, on expediency but also on the belief that Russia can offer something new, a redesigned secular state that can compete with the previous anti-religious separation of the USSR, or what Hurd refers to as the dominant separationist-laicite models (Hurd 2008).

In this instance, the ecclesiastical hierarchy is granted some limited influence within the ruling structure, and the sociological dominance of one tradition is recognised as such. The Russian Orthodox Church and the Transition to Democracy (1985-2000) There is ample evidence that religion has played a significant role in supporting the overthrow of authoritarian governments and the shift to democracy. The majority of research conducted in Southern Europe, Latin America, Africa, or Asia on religion and regime change focuses on the ways in which religious actors criticise social injustice and violations of human rights in public or offer symbolic outlets for resistance like pilgrimages, holy sites, and funerals. They emphasise the role that religion plays in mediating disputes between the ruling party and the opposition, as well as in institutionally defending civil society and offering alternative forums for discussion and debate.

However, religion played a very small role in the USSR, with the possible exception of the mostly Catholic Lithuania. Orthodox hierarchs in the Russian heartland remained mute, neither publicly criticising the status quo nor actively supporting civil society. While there were a few religious dissidents, many of them were imprisoned when Gorbachev took office. A few of them were also involved in political activities and efforts to uphold the human rights guarantees outlined in the Soviet Constitution. It would be difficult to argue that there was a distinctly institutional religious contribution to the developing civil society movements once he began freeing prisoners of conscience at the end of 1986. So, despite the lofty claims occasionally made for the role of religion in the wider collapse of communism, with particular attention to the role of Pope John Paul II, the simple answer here is to say that there was no significant role of religion in the Soviet Union (Weigel 1992).

Having said that, it's possible that religion's continued existence at all following 70 years of enforced secularisation contributed in a less evident way to the grassroots revolution of the regime. A general discontent with the regime that was difficult to voice in public was fueled by small groups of intellectuals, artists, and others becoming involved with the religious philosophy of the turn of the century, growing awareness of religious debates in the West, and the examination of religious themes in published and unpublished literature during the 1960s and 1970s. Furthermore, the persistence of religious beliefs and practices among segments of the populace—often markedly distorted, tangentially linked to the official doctrine of the churches, and occasionally grouped together under the heading of "folk religion"—contributed to a partial undermining of the legitimacy of the system.

Although assessing this effect is highly challenging and varies greatly across regions, it undoubtedly played a part in the somewhat nascent state of preparedness for change that Gorbachev could expand upon. Russian Orthodox leaders had to establish a position for themselves in the new political order only after the fall of the Soviet Union, and even then, they had to do so in a situation that showed that transition was not a straight line with a democratic conclusion. Boris Yeltsin assumed leadership of the newly formed Russian Federation after Mikhail Gorbachev left the Kremlin, stripping it of its larger empire. The talk at the time was all about Russia becoming a "normal" power in the international order, establishing a free market economy, and advancing democracy and civil society.

Less was known about what democracy actually meant, as politicians holding wildly divergent opinions all claimed the mantle while maybe not fully grasping its implications. Preventing a communist return and averting an economic collapse were the president's and those around him's top priorities. In the years that followed, it became clear that they were not too picky about the methods employed. If pressed to justify these methods, they would argue that developing a functional democracy would be impossible without guaranteeing these two objectives. The fall of the previous government inexorably brought with it new difficulties for religious leaders. Even if they had contributed to the shift, this was probably going to diminish over time as new social actors like political parties, pressure groups, social movements, etc. appeared. They may not have enjoyed the previous government, but they occasionally missed the discipline and moral rectitude of authoritarianism. They also viewed democracy and pluralism as having an "anything goes" mentality. Although they acknowledged and endorsed the discourse, the leaders of the Russian Orthodox Church did not view democracy as a top priority. In actuality, though, their top concerns were rebuilding the churches and other institutions that had been largely abandoned in earlier decades, recruiting enough people to meet the population's religious needs, and educating a flock that, for the most part, knew very little about the religious doctrine, moral instruction, and worship of the church (Anderson 1994: 137-214; Ellis 1996). Church leaders expressed early concerns about what some referred to as the "invasion of the sects" and were relieved to see state control return, but they were less happy about the ways in which this opened up the religious market (Witte and Bourdeaux 1999).

As the so-called church of the majority and the "traditional" religion, they felt that they should have a special place in the new political order, even though they did not expressly oppose religious freedom. The idea that Russia should return to its true path as an Orthodox nation was central to the church's understanding of the political changes of the late 1980s and early 1990s, and it fit in well with the country's growing rejection of the idea that it should just follow Western models, which was infused with nationalism. The church's main goal was for church and state to work together, but without the subjugation that characterised the late Tsarist and Soviet eras. Although church and state were legally distinct, the church leadership managed to end inquiries into their previous cooperation with the Soviet government, establish a presence at all significant state events, and eventually retrieve some of the property that had been lost during the Soviet era.

In a 1997 interview, Patriarch Aleksii acknowledged that the state and the church should be kept apart, but he contended that the church could not be completely cut off from society and the people (Interview with Patriarch Aleksii 1997). However, in actuality, church-state relations were presumably closer than in many European states with surviving established churches, and in 2013, calls for a formal constitutional acknowledgment of Orthodoxy's superiority began to emerge. The church never enjoyed exclusive privileging, as proposed by Koesel (Koesel 2014: 167), and it was never able to be classified as "hegemonic" according to Cesari. Rather, religious communities that fit the definition of "traditional" in Russia—that is, highly associated with particular ethnic groups within the Russian Federation—were expected to embrace "hierarchical pluralism," as defined by Agadjanian. This strategy was "founded on an understanding of Orthodoxy (the faith of the Moscow Patriarchate and the Russian Orthodox Church) as the standard of religious life, appropriate to the goals of the state and the aspirations of the people." The evaluation of all other religions was based on how close they were to this standard and how well they could interact with it. This resulted in the formation of a hierarchy of faiths, which is the hierarchy of symbolic congruence with national identity (Agadjanian 2000: 119-20). Within this framework, Orthodoxy held a dominant position, with Islam, Judaism, Buddhism, and Christian denominations associated with specific ethnic groups following suit. Beneath them were a variety of groups, including the Baptists, who were occasionally accepted with reluctance, as well as neo-Pentecostals, Jehovah's Witnesses, Hare Krishnas, and Scientologists, all of whom were written off as "sects" with no real claim to a place in the emerging Russian religious landscape (Fagan 2012). A number of significant events in the 1990s and beyond indicated this shift towards a closer relationship with the state, including attempts to impose restrictions on religious pluralism, criticise the liberal-democratic nexus, advocate for a specific form of religious education in schools, and assert the right to exercise moral guardianship over the broader society.

Church leaders were extremely wary of the demands of a democratic polity because they lacked experience with them and understood little about how they would affect their own interests. Their upbringing in the Soviet Union contributed to their tendency to be defensive and wary of independent social action, similar to other organisations. However, their internal hierarchical structure and necessity to adhere to a traditionalist and conservative theology in order to withstand persecution during the Soviet era may have made them more cautious than others. Church leaders in Russia were unfamiliar with the workings of a democratic government and frequently felt more at ease working with the political figures they had collaborated with before 1991. As fervently conservative men, they were wary of social pluralism that appeared to be legal, and they looked to the government for assistance in reining in the worst excesses in the social and religious spheres. One can evaluate their contribution to democratisation by looking at how they functioned in the domains of civil and political society, whether they demonstrated a willingness to accept a certain amount of social and political pluralism, and whether they promoted tolerance and acceptance of difference. At the highest levels of leadership, the church has favoured exerting its political influence through working inside the corridors of power. In this capacity, it has questioned the viability of liberal democracy in Russia, appeared to reject the idea of universal human rights, and taken the lead in efforts to restrict the rights of religious minorities and, more recently, in advocating for other illiberal policies. Although it was evident that the church was functioning in a post-2000 political environment where democracy in any meaningful sense was not a priority, this was further supported by its choice to play a supportive role for the Kremlin rather than adopt a "prophetic" or pro-democratic one. While we will discuss some of these topics again later, for the time being, we only address the issue of religious pluralism. In an effort to limit entry into the religious marketplace, the relatively liberal freedom of conscience law of the Gorbachev era was changed in the 1990s, marking the first significant political muscle-flexing by Orthodox hierarchs. The result of this was a new law that was approved by the State Duma in 1997. Its preamble granted the Russian Orthodox Church a symbolic advantage while dividing religious organisations into three different categories according to their rights and recognition. Although the concept was not used, it served as the foundation for the concept of "traditional religions," which was later extensively used by the Orthodox Church and government representatives (Fagan 2012: 121-51). Even though it's frequently viewed as the one big success of Orthodox lobbying in the 1990s, Irina Papkova correctly notes that it was largely the result of a specific environment in which church goals aligned with a strong anti-Western sentiment among the political elite.

This sentiment resulted from the perception that the outside world hadn't provided the expected level of financial support for Russian "reforms" and from some Western political leaders' presumption that the new Russia should just adopt their political, economic, and foreign policy agendas. This was also seen in the religious arena in the middle of the 1990s, when religious and secular leaders attacked "the invasion of the sects" in an often-hysterical anti-sect campaign in the Russian media. Though many of these groups had been in Russia for decades, if not centuries, there was a tendency to portray virtually all "unknown" religious minorities—from Hare Krishnas to most Protestants—as the product of lavishly funded US and European missionary groups (Papkova 2011: 74-93; Anderson 2003: 115-38). The 1997 law's details were interpreted differently as the new century drew closer. It was probably accurate to state that although the law did not return Russia to its Soviet past, certain groups did suffer from severe harassment and restrictions and still do. 4 In terms of democratisation, this law was significant because it conveyed to the general public that differences should not be welcomed or celebrated but rather should be viewed as threats. Subsequently, there were several attempts to further tighten the law, limit evangelism, and outlaw certain groups under "anti-extremist" legislation.

These efforts further served to "securitize" other religious groups, such as many Muslim groups, some Protestant groups, and other groups deemed to be "sects" that posed a threat to Russian security. Though mostly content to overlook the ongoing persecution of organisations like Jehovah's Witnesses, some Pentecostal groups, unofficial Muslim communities, and others grouped together as "sects" or labelled as "extremists," the Kremlin seemed content with the changes made in 1997 and unwilling to support further legal restrictions (Fagan 2012: 155-71). The Bases of the Social Concept of the Russian Orthodox Church and The Basic Principles of Attitudes to the NonOrthodox are two important documents published by the Council of Bishops in 2000 that are helpful in understanding the Russian Church's stance on religious freedom. In the first, the argument for the value of freedom of conscience was that it allowed the church to continue operating in a secular society.

However, in Russia, this argument was further supported by the fact that the country had "lost its religious goals and values and became massively apostate" (Social Concept 2000), which is hardly a glowing recommendation. In the later document, the basic assertion that "the Orthodox Church is the true Church of Christ" (1.1) was made first, followed by the more direct assertion that "all other institutions claiming to be churches have moved away from the Orthodox, and true unification is possible only in the bosom of the One, Holy, Catholic, and Apostolic

Church" (2.3). Because of this, the Church (2.7) cannot adopt any model of interchurch relations that presumes the equality of all denominations, and consequently, the state should not provide equal support to all. It recognises the right of non-Orthodox communities to testify to their faith within the borders of the former Soviet Union, but only in relation to "population groups that traditionally belong to them" (6.3). It will cooperate with churches that share traditional creedal commitments. Claims that the church is the only true Christian church and that Russia is its "canonical territory" and that minorities have the right to work only among people who "belong to them" (Basic Principles 2000) further exacerbate the tendency to be suspicious of religious pluralism. It is pretty obvious to the Church's leadership that pluralism based on equal freedom for all must inevitably be limited and that freedom of conscience has to be qualified by the historically dominant Orthodox tradition. From 2000 to 2011, towards a new "symphonia"? The scene was set for change when Vladimir Putin officially assumed office as president in early 2000. He had come to power on the platform of bringing pride and order back to a Russia battered by the fall of the empire, social and economic collapse, and political instability. He developed a system of what became known as "managed," later "sovereign," democracy over the ensuing years. It was marketed as a model better suited to Russian cultural conditions, and in practice, it meant that elections were held but that parties or individuals with Kremlin support won.

Voting was allowed, and officially backed candidates might occasionally lose, but in an environment where public space and media freedom were being restricted, electoral fraud was a common occurrence, and there were significant organisational barriers for those trying to establish legitimate opposition movements—apart from the shortcomings of those who aspired to such a role. Formally, this regime could be characterised as "hybrid," but it was leaning more and more towards authoritarianism, and the lack of real "feedback" from society meant that the Kremlin was unprepared for the level of popular unrest that surfaced in 2011-12. (Petrov, Lipman, and Hale 2014: 17-21). This top-down stabilisation system had to be preferable to the circumstances of the previous ten years for many people, and this was undoubtedly the case for church leaders who were enamoured with a leader who identified as an Orthodox believer and showed appropriate respect for religious institutions. Although there was doubt about his dedication to genuinely democratic principles, church leaders were not particularly concerned about it. While they made it apparent that there was a difference in the relationship between the state and the Russian Orthodox Church, they still denied any desire to become a state church (Interview with Metropolitan Hilarion 2010).

Orthodox leaders occasionally saw this as offering a distinctively Russian way of being "secular." Church spokesmen increasingly preferred to speak off this as a return to something akin to the Byzantine notion of symphonia, where each side had distinct but entwined roles; others argued for a more theocratic perspective along the lines of the Old Testament judges, where the political and religious leadership could occasionally be provided by the same person (Social Concept 2000; Anderson 2009: 133-38 & 144-45). Although Patriarch Kirill stated in a March 2011 broadcast that it would be improper for the church to get involved in politics, he did suggest that the church could still have an impact by promoting the Christian message and offering moral assessments. As for the state, it was pleased to grant symbolic recognition, as demonstrated by the Patriarch's move back into the Kremlin in November 2011 and his occupation of the rooms once occupied by church leaders in bygone ages (Okorokova 2011).

Since there isn't enough room to go into detail about the complex dynamics of church-state relations at this time (Know 2004; Papkova 2011; Fagan 2012), we will instead concentrate on Orthodox perspectives on issues pertaining to democracy and human rights. During this time, it became evident that democracy was not the sole option available in the Russian Federation, and concerns regarding the Russian Orthodox Church's dedication to democracy were not unfounded. Many academics have argued that religious traditions are multivocal and that all of them can and have adapted to democratic traditions; however, it's also possible that, depending on the situation, what I've called a tradition's "centre of gravity" could act in a way that either helps or hinders the development of democratic polities (Stepan 2000; Anderson 2004). It is debatable why traditions "shift," with some emphasising the significance of local contextual factors; others focus on theological and ideological change (Catholicism's Vatican II); others on the necessity of maintaining social hegemony or market share. In the case of Russia, the writings and speeches of influential religious figures demonstrate a strong scepticism, if not outright rejection, of liberal conceptions of democracy and the assertion that these conceptions have their roots in a universally accepted understanding of human rights. Instead, we witness what is, in theory, a perfectly legitimate attempt by the Moscow Patriarchate and the Kremlin to create an authentic Russian vision of democracy, which is paralleled in a few Muslim debates about democracy. However, some may wonder what remains of democracy in this particular conception, the details of which have not yet been clarified.

The church's leadership created a social critique in the late 1990s and early 21st century that was based on a strong mistrust of and animosity towards the liberalism they perceived as being peculiar to Western societies and out of step with Russian culture. The basic contradiction of our era, according to Metropolitan Kirill's widely cited 2000 argument, "is the opposition of liberal civilised standards on the one hand and the values of national, cultural, and religious identity on the other" (Patriarch Kirill 2000). We are unable to go into great detail about this at this time. The future Patriarch and his colleagues believed that the liberal emphasis on unrestricted individual freedom ignored any concept of sin or that people are "unique human persons" situated in specific communities, nor that people's actions should generally conform to the standards and moral values of those communities (Agadjanian & Rousselet 2005). Their opposition to the notion that Western European standards ought to be portrayed as universal and binding on Russia fit in well with the Kremlin's developing conception of "sovereign democracy." Prominent religious spokespersons seemed to go along with the Putin administration's less democratic moves. One of the main public relations spokespersons for the Moscow Patriarchate, Fr. Vsevolod Chaplin described democracy as a system of government that "rejects religious authority and declares the government independent from God...it is rooted in competition." According to Chaplin, the Church views the nation as a living organism, a unified body that views disagreements as unhealthy. Chaplin wrote this in an article published in 2004. Furthermore, the church should prioritise "uniting its forces in service to the fatherland and the nation" over "democratic development" (Chaplin 2004: 31-46). By 2007, he had become much more antagonistic, saying things like "multi-confessionality, multiparty systems, separation of powers, competition, administrative conflicts—all that the present political system takes such pride in—are symptoms of spiritual unhealthiness." He also implied that "Orthodox civilization stands in opposition to western democracy, whose downfall is not far off." No, sin is the primary cause of a pluralistic democracy's very existence. Fr. Chaplin believed that by lowering political squabbling and transforming parliament into a venue for the "harmonisation of interests," the Russian government had made progress towards the right goals (Zaitseva 2007). Metropolitan Kirill made similar remarks, speaking more and more of a unique Russian civilization in which the idea of sovereign democracy was far more suited to the nation's culture than the clamorous competition and self-serving pursuit of interests that he perceived to be hallmarks of democratic politics in most of Europe and North America. The Church's views on human rights were likewise ambivalent, as they tried to address the issue of what would take the place of liberalism and pluralism, beginning with the idea that the autonomous individual ought to be the central concern of any system of rights.

A Russian Declaration of Human Rights was created in 2006 with assistance from the Church for the World Council of the Russian People's annual meeting. This document emphasised the prior right of "internal freedom from evil and the right of moral choice," describing itself as speaking for the "distinct Russian civilization" (Filatov 2012a: 14). Kirill frequently seemed to use this concept as much as any narrowly religious understanding of Russia. According to this view, morality and human rights were inextricably linked, and the declaration acknowledged that values such as "faith, morality, and the sanctity of holy objects and one's homeland" were equally significant to human rights.

Therefore, it was imperative to guarantee that the exercise of individual rights did not infringe upon religious or moral traditions or offend religious or national sentiments. Additionally, it mentioned how the church and the state worked together to "preserve the rights of nations and ethnic groups to their individual religion," though it was not entirely clear what this meant in terms of people's freedom to practice any religion they choose. In an interview from April 2006, Metropolitan Kirill made the argument that the liberal interpretation of human rights was growing more assertive and attempting to project a universal image in the West. According to him, the Western understanding of rights developed independently of traditional religious beliefs, as though morality could not be brought up when discussing rights (Interview with Patriarch Kirill, 2006).

When Kirill highlighted some of the implications of the Church's position in a speech to the UN Human Rights Council in March 2008, he created a stir by stating: "The human rights approach has been...used to justify the outrage against and distortion of religious symbols and teachings." Today, the same method is used to force schools to teach a 14-day course on introduction to various religions rather than the fundamentals of their own. In addition, extreme feminist ideologies and homosexual attitudes have a significant influence on the creation of policies, guidelines, and programmes related to human rights advocacy, which are detrimental to the institution of the family and population reproduction. The Russian Orthodox Church remained unapologetic despite the UN Council subcommittee issuing a critical minute after he attacked the relativistic approach to human rights, which should be implemented "taking into account the cultural distinctive features of a particular people" (Blitt 2011: 406-10). As per a church representative, the initial comprehension of human rights was rooted in the Christian perception of the human being, which, although possessing inalienable rights, functions within a moral agreement. This is evident in the context of the family, wherein the Christian interpretation of matrimony was accepted as evident to all. The Christian right to religious freedom was first recognised in tandem with the declaration of individual human rights. But over time, significant changes occurred in both Europe and the global community. Furthermore, when a wholly secular perspective on human rights took hold in European (in the cultural sense) societies, a whole new scenario emerged. "All human beings are born free and equal in dignity and rights," states Article I of the 1948 Universal Declaration of Human Rights.

They ought to behave kindly towards one another because they are endowed with conscience and reason. The creator is no longer mentioned at all. Nowadays, a biological understanding of human nature, as opposed to a religious one, forms the foundation of natural law. Simultaneously, the contemporary notion of human rights, in opposition to different ideologies of exclusivity on a national or cultural level, was founded upon the ideology of liberal individualism, which originated in Western Europe but asserted its universality (Bulekov 2007). A further revised document that echoed many of these concerns was accepted by the Bishop's Council of the Moscow Patriarchate in June 2008. It added that "civilizations should not impose their lifestyle patterns on other civilizations" or "serve the interests of certain countries" under the guise of protecting human rights. Kristina Stoeckl argues that this stance may be taken to contribute in a distinctively Orthodox way to the discussion of rights while simultaneously acknowledging that different people may have different interpretations of what constitutes a right (Stoeckl 2011: 217-33). She does not, however, necessarily mean that the church is rejecting the possibility of a universal conception of human rights.

Simultaneously, the church's stance seemed to resemble the outdated Soviet constitution, implying that exercising one's rights required adhering to socialist principles, which are now considered religious. According to Alexander Agadjanian, this document implied that the Russian Orthodox leadership was rejecting "not only the excesses of individualism but altogether the very notion of the autonomous individual as the holder of inalienable rights" and asserting "religious, moral, and cultural hegemony" (Agadjanian 2010: 104-6). Church and state in perfect harmony, 2012-2015 During a large portion of the first decade of the twenty-first century, the Church's leadership made great efforts to mend its differences with the initial Putin administrations (2000-2008). They hoped that this seemingly Orthodox president would support their ambitions for a larger role in public life, but they had no desire to be subservient. The fact that church and state differed on certain issues contributed to the difficulty of this relationship at times. Putin allegedly wanted Pope John Paul II to visit Russia in spite of church opposition, referred to Russia as a multi-confessional state multiple times, and showed ambivalence towards Orthodox-based religious instruction in schools.

Dmitry Medvedev (2008-212) oversaw the approval of a law pertaining to the return of church property, the introduction of significantly modified religious studies courses in public schools, and the implementation of programmes to supply military chaplains in the armed forces. When those in positions of authority made bolder statements, like Vladislav Surkov, the Kremlin spin doctor, who declared in the middle of 2011 that "Putin was given to Russia by God and destiny in a hard hour for our one big nation," the church was cautious about lending too much support to them. Fr. Vsevolod Chaplin, the patriarchal spokesman, replied that it was premature to assess the accomplishments of the current administration, but he did hope that Putin and Medvedev had been sent for a reason (Interfax religii, July 12 and 19, 2011). Public demonstrations in the run-up to the 2011-12 elections were going to put this relationship to the test even further. While the church hierarchy stayed silent at first, several priests and theologians started to express their concerns about the election results via social media and church publications. Fr. Feodor Lyudogovsky asserted that there was substantial proof of ballot stuffing and statistical manipulation by election officials, and he suggested that the 16th election was conducted under intense administrative pressure.

Although he voiced doubts regarding certain intense discussions surrounding the parliamentary elections, he proposed that lies and hypocrisy typified the elections as a whole (Lyugovsky 2011). On their Facebook pages, other priests criticised the election process, shared their experiences participating in protests, and detailed instances of electoral fraud in specific districts (Melnikov 2011). The Moscow Patriarchate was unprepared for all of this and found it difficult to react. The head of the Synodal Information Department, Vladimir Legoida, first urged people to remain calm and reported any evidence of significant electoral fraud to the church's Department of Church-Society Relations. Public affairs spokesperson Fr. Vsevolod Chaplin backed this stance, stating that they would be prepared to pursue any verified infractions with the government's electoral commission (Kishkovsky 2011). Patriarch Kirill, for his part, advised caution and emphasised the need to maintain a strong state in a Christmas interview. He also cautioned protestors not to be used by those vying for political power, thereby endorsing the Kremlin line that protests are all the product of a tiny minority and not a reflection of genuine grievances. He reminded his audience of how the Soviet Union was overthrown by protests at the end of the 1980s and how the Bolsheviks hijacked the 1917 revolution to impose oppressive rule (BBC Online, January 7, 2012).

Some were more vocal than others; Skhiarchimandrite Ilii, Kirill's spiritual father, implied that those 'who hate our country' were behind the protests and that their goal was to incite social unrest in Russia (Filatov 2012b). The controversy surrounding the Pussy Riot demonstration in the Cathedral of Christ the Saviour only served to incite the Church to rally behind the president, which did not help the Moscow Patriarchate maintain composure. By mid-February, the Patriarch had abandoned his earlier call for increased communication and transparency, as Kirill referred to Putin as a "miracle of God" and those in his immediate vicinity demanded an end to demonstrations that endangered the stability of the nation and its citizens. Fr. Chaplin stated that "the power of this personality is obvious, and the popular trust is obvious, which is of a length unprecedented in the history of Russian democracy" in response to President Putin's reelection (Moshin 2012). For primarily self-serving reasons, church and state have gotten closer since the 2011-12 election scandals. Both groups' leaders have acted to punish community members who were overly vocal during the protests, harbour a suspicion of autonomous 17 social action and organisation in their respective domains, and have pushed for a more nationalistic emphasis on Russia's right to forge its own course in development. This has also made it more advantageous for the church hierarchy to lobby for support of its own agenda, most notably for laws that would outlaw "propaganda of non-traditional sexual relations" and support legislation that would restrict access to abortion. Following the Pussy Riot incident, they applauded the enactment of legislation safeguarding believers' religious sentiments.

While the targeting of homosexuals may spark outrage from other countries, the "blasphemy law," which aims to prevent a repeat of the Pussy Riot-style incidents and deter those responsible for the 2012 vandalism of religious sites and symbols, has somewhat less support from the general public. Towards the close of 2013, a few lawmakers suggested going one step further and amending the 1993 Constitution. The head of the Duma's Committee on Family, Women, and Children, Elena Mizulina, proposed a change to the preamble of the constitution that would highlight the role that Orthodoxy played in the formation of Russian history. The appeal from multiple public organisations, which claimed that "Orthodoxy is the national idea of Russia, its special civilizational code, and the essence of its spiritual sovereignty," served as the foundation for this proposal. The foundation of Russian identity is Orthodoxy. We therefore urge that the spiritual sovereignty of the Russian Federation be recognised by the

Russian constitution, which acknowledges the unique role of Orthodoxy in the same way that legislation confirms the governmental sovereignty of the Russian Federation, while emphasising that this does not violate the rights of minorities (Interfax religii, 25 November 2013). Church leaders endorsed this idea, and in January 2015, Patriarch Kirill was invited to address parliament, seemingly acknowledging the church's de facto growing influence.

He made use of the occasion to advocate for legislative restrictions on abortion and to uphold traditional values. He went on to say that "the idea of prioritising the value of free choice and rejecting the priority of moral norms has become a slow-acting bomb for Western civilization," defending Russia's unique historical tradition (Radio Free Europe 2015). Church, state, and democratization (18) A large portion of the literature on democratisation emphasises the tension that exists between the state and religion as religious organisations, for various reasons, come to support their countries' democratic processes and, as a result, find themselves at odds with the authoritarian government. Concurrently, there is a debate about whether some religious traditions are intrinsically democratic or not, which is mostly pointless and frequently historical. Recent research has concentrated on the institutional dynamic and the ways in which interactions between the state and religion can influence political evolution and move religious traditions and organisations in the direction of democracy. "Islam is not antidemocratic per se, but certain forms of state-religion interaction, such as regulating, restricting, or privileging religious activity," according to Jocelyne Cesari's study on

Muslim democracy (Cesari 2014: 15). In contrast to the religion-state conflict frequently connected to political transitions, Karrie Koesel contends in her research on religion and authoritarianism in China and Russia that "the nature of the contemporary authoritarian project...provides incentives for collaboration" (Koesel 2014: 28). This article's main argument is that the Kremlin's political elite has not made creating a clearly democratic state in Russia a top priority, preferring to focus on creating a strong state. Under these conditions, the Russian Orthodox Church hierarchy has shown itself incapable of advancing democratisation or unwilling to do so. The church's senior leaders were often appointed during the Soviet era, so part of the reason for their reluctance may be that they have never worked in a democratic or pluralist environment. However, there is no proof that younger bishops are more likely to have pro-democratic views.

Additionally, Orthodoxy is assumed to be the predominant religion in Russia, and some hierarchies aspire to a position that is comparable to Cesari's concept of hegemonic religion. In addition, there is an ideological-theological viewpoint that is based on the idea that Russian civilization is unique and that democratic, or otherwise, forms of government should be derived from (presumably fixed) Russian cultural traditions rather than the liberal individualism that is supposed to be the foundation of liberal democracy in North America and Europe. This stems from a poorly expressed fear that, in a society still healing from decades of coerced anti-religion, pluralism could be a sign of increased societal secularisation. Even though these influences have an impact on how church leaders think, they still have options, and other factors may have been involved in this decision. The 19 incentives almost entirely work against democratisation in Russia, which has a lot to do with the changing dynamics between church and state. In contrast, major religious institutions in parts of Latin America and Africa may have been pressured to support democratisation due to a combination of theological change, religious competition, and vested interests. Until recently, Russia's post-communist government welcomed religious institutions' support and found its symbols useful for general legitimation and the creation of a new Russian identity. For its part, the church saw the state as an almost natural ally in its struggle to establish religious authority in the new Russia. Since the 2011-12 election crisis, the younger, more educated segments of the urban population—some of whom were beginning to doubt the Kremlin's authority to select leaders on its behalf—have put pressure on the Putin administration to cultivate support bases more actively and urgently than it had in the past. It has viewed the Russian Orthodox Church as an obvious ally in these circumstances, and as such, it has been more willing to back church-backed positions on issues such as abortion rights, gay rights, the protection of believers' sentiments, and even the prospect of granting the church a formal, if symbolic, constitutional status. As a result, the church leadership has sharpened its support for church-state cooperation and grown even more acquiescent to Putin's government.

It seems that neither partner is particularly interested in democracy in this cooperative arrangement. Many states define democracy using a qualifier, such as "liberal," "socialist," "Islamic," or even "basic," as in the case of Pakistan under General Ayub Khan. However, the Russian model is different from the latter because, according to the Kremlin, "sovereign democracy" is a fully democratic model that is suitable for Russian conditions, while Ayub Khan seemed to accept that there was a core (Western) model and that Pakistan was not ready for this fullyfledged democratic system.

In addition, one could contend that, in actuality, the Russian Church is more like an established church than the Church of England in the English portion of the United Kingdom because, even with Russia's formal symbolic and representational roles and the separation of church and state, the Anglican church has less overt policy influence than the Russian church leadership has had in the last five years. The limitations of formal models of church-state relations are thus brought to our attention. Three Russian Orthodox leaders like to portray Russia as a nation where religious minorities are treated equally and there is only one dominant religion, but in actuality, Russia is a multi-religious society with a dominant religion. Despite the fact that surveys show that about 70% of people identify as "Orthodox," religious observance and practice are extremely low, and about half of those who regularly attend worship are located in non-Orthodox locations. Approximately 10% of the population is Muslim by ethnicity; they are primarily restricted to specific areas, though there are sizable communities of migrant workers in the Moscow and St. Petersburg regions. Additionally, there are sizable populations of Roman Catholics, Buddhists, Jews, and various Protestant and charismatic groups; some sources claim that the latter group's active members outnumber the Orthodox in Siberia and the Russian Far East. Additionally, there are a variety of Western and indigenous religious groups that are commonly referred to as "sects" by the media and other religious groups. While there will be some political interactions and representation on various administrative bodies among all of these, when it comes to access to political elites both at the national level and in many of the regions, the Russian Orthodox Church is unquestionably primus inter pares.

It is the only religious organization whose leaders have addressed democracy extensively, if mostly negatively.

3.5 Russia's Regime Change Won't Cause Pandemonium or Collapse

History demonstrates that in Russia, changes in leadership have nearly invariably been followed by liberalization rather than civil unrest.

The post-Putin era will begin when President Vladimir Putin leaves office, whatever that may be. There is a great deal of uncertainty surrounding this next chapter in Russian history, and many people are afraid of what it might bring: maybe Russia will fall apart or become unstable, or maybe a more brutal leader will emerge.

The events of this summer, when Wagner leader Yevgeny Prigozhin launched his brief rebellion, seemed to confirm such ominous predictions. The subsequent military conflict, however, was not indicative of anarchy; rather, the leaders of the uprising soon met their demise, and those who supported it either defected or vanished into the vastness of Russia.

The Russian elite was forced to step up their efforts to show their allegiance to Putin after the uprising because suspicions were high. Simultaneously, the majority of Russians continued to be interested in nothing more than being left in peace to carry on with their lives. It appears sufficient to show imitation loyalty to the regime for those who have not been swept up in the mobilisation or who would rather not volunteer for the front.

Attempting to terrify the world by projecting the image of a leader worse than Putin is strange. What could be more oppressive in Russia than the Soviet Union's final years and the largest military confrontation in Europe of the twenty-first century? We already live in an anti-Utopia because of the Kremlin and a cowardly elite.

Who is this monster of the future who would dethrone Putin? Maybe the notoriously hawkish head of the Security Council, Nikolai Patrushev? Is he, however, worse than Putin? He is merely one representative of the current government, a mouthpiece for conspiracy theories and anti-American sentiment.

Would it be worse to have a general like the late Prigozhin? First of all, Prigozhin would not have been well-known had he not been supported by the Putin apparatus, given billions of state funds, and developed into the most skilled independent contractor in the Kremlin. Second, in order to pose a significant threat to the authorities, you must possess his charm, financial resources, and insider knowledge. Such people are just no longer in existence.

Can a coup occur? The political culture does not support it. To believe that a conspiracy is the most likely scenario would be to take mass protests over declining living standards seriously.

It is crucial to keep in mind that the modern police state would quickly put an end to any significant anti-Putin Street demonstration. It would probably end even faster than what happened on January 25, 1968, when eight protesters against the Soviet invasion of Czechoslovakia were arrested by police on Red Square. That's precisely the message the authorities are sending people today. One of the police officers who detained dissident Pavel Litvinov that day said something that would go down in history: "You fool—if you'd stayed at home, you'd have lived a peaceful life."

And the social fabric of Russia is not falling apart, even in an anti-Utopia. The nation's economic system has held steady in spite of all the issues. The capacity for adaptation in Russian society was undervalued; in addition to the general public's apathy towards political developments, this capacity helps guarantee the authorities at least some degree of support.

An orderly transition to a new regime in Russia will be aided by the general lack of interest among the populace, which will submit to any legitimate ruler. Once power shifts occur, beloved Putin won't be so beloved anymore. It has always been that way.

Furthermore, if we look at previous instances, liberalisation rather than violent chaos has nearly always accompanied Russian leadership changes (think of Khrushchev's thawing after Stalin, Gorbachev's perestroika following Brezhnev's gerontocracy, and Yeltsin's reforms following the fall of the Soviet Union). Historically, power struggles, even at the top, have not always resulted in chaos.

Remarkably, Russia did not experience extremely severe instability following the fall of the Soviet Union. The majority of people were preoccupied with surviving, making adjustments, and—above all—using the new opportunities. It is true that in October 1993, the nation saw a brief civil war as a result of a struggle between the president and the parliament. However, the majority chose to remain neutral and support the victorious side. To put it briefly, there is no evidence that the impending power shift in Russia—which is inevitable—will result in either chaos or a more authoritarian government.

Some analysts also use Russia's disintegration as a bogeyman. However, this is even less likely than civil unrest or the rise of a leader who is even less capable than Putin. Russia's early 1990s rush for sovereignty resulted from regions trying to survive while facing the challenges of building new state institutions and an economy. When we look back on the 1990s, we frequently overlook the enormous obstacles the government faced, such as empty coffers and a lack of state agencies and bureaucracy.

Russia will not collapse in the post-Putin era for strong economic, budgetary, and political management reasons.

Russia is not an especially wealthy nation, and regional disparity exacerbates wealth inequality, leaving many areas in need of government assistance. To put it briefly, regional economies are unable to thrive on their own, and exiting the Russian Federation would present significant challenges.

If regional leaders are interested in independence, it is limited to Russia's national republics. However, as previously mentioned, the majority of these countries receive political support in exchange for maintaining social order, and it is not by accident that funding for the occupied Crimean port city of Sevastopol increased by 54% in the first half of 2023.

Furthermore, regional leaders have become technocrats in recent years, closely supervised by the federal centre in everything they do. They are completely reliant on Moscow and answerable to the Kremlin rather than the local populace. Instead of becoming strong local leaders, all these regional leaders hope to land a prestigious position in the federal government.

The Kremlin deserves credit for its achievements in establishing a system staffed by obedient technocrats who regard themselves as temporary supervisors who are subject to arbitrary firing. This serves as a safeguard against local separatism.

If Putin is replaced by a technocrat, that power transition scenario is comparatively optimistic. His replacement is not guaranteed; candidates for the position include Dmitry Patrushev, the son of Patrushev, the leader of United Russia; Andrei Turchak; Speaker of the State

Duma Vyacheslav Volodin; and Sergei Kiriyenko, the deputy chief of staff of the Kremlin. It could just as easily be Moscow Mayor Sergei Sobyanin or Prime Minister Mikhail Mishustin, who are ranked second in Russia's trustworthiness rankings by Levada Centre polling. Both Mishustin and Sobyanin have made an effort to maintain their standing as practical managers.

Given that Putin's model of governance is gradually and inevitably wearing thin on all fronts—financially, socially, economically, psychologically, and politically—a technocratic or interim leader will have to be able to facilitate the shift towards normalisation. Nothing could possibly be worse.

Beijing and Xi Jinping

Similar to this, Xi Jinping has led China for an extended period of time while holding the positions of President and General Secretary of the Communist Party. A Christian analysis of his leadership raises the following issues:

Restricted Political Diversity

Under Xi Jinping, the political environment in China is characterised by restricted political pluralism, with the Chinese Communist Party retaining a firm grip on power. From a Christian perspective, accountability and checks and balances are essential, and they may be hampered by a noncompetitive political environment.

Religious Minorities Persecuted

China's treatment of religious minorities, particularly Christians, has drawn criticism. Christians who respect religious freedom and empathy for the persecuted have expressed concern over reports of church closures, religious persecution, and human rights violations.

Power concentration

The elimination of term limits for presidents has been a hallmark of Xi Jinping's consolidation of power, further centralising power. The Christian values of humility and accountability may be called into question by this concentration of power.

Repression of Opposition

More restrictions on civil society and freedom of speech have been put in place under Xi's direction, and this includes the silencing of critical voices. The repression of dissent is incompatible with Christian values of compassion, justice, and the value of free and open discourse.

Change is needed

From a Christian standpoint, there are numerous strong arguments in favor of regular changes in the government's leadership:

Responsibility

A shift in leadership offers a chance to hold leaders responsible for their choices and actions. Being accountable is essential to Christian leadership because it is expected of leaders to act morally and justly.

Novel Perspectives

Novel viewpoints and concepts are presented by newly appointed leaders. This can be especially helpful in addressing changing problems and coming up with creative fixes. Leadership stagnation can impede development and adaptation.

Lowliness

A change in leadership can aid in halting the rise of haughtiness and conceit. One of the most important Christian virtues is humility, which leaders should demonstrate through their choices and actions.

Fairness and emotion

A shift in authority may bring justice and compassion back to the forefront, especially for disadvantaged and vulnerable populations. Christian values place a high value on assisting the poor and advancing social justice.

3.6 The implications of Xi Jinping's third term for the world

Through Michael Schuman

The inner workings of Chinese politics at the highest levels are opaque. Similar to former Kremlinologists, those who observe China are compelled to comb through People's Daily front pages and dinner party gossip to find out who's in and who's out. Up until they are announced at Chinese Communist Party congresses every five years, the winners of China's political backroom battles are never known. It is amazing that China's political system is still so opaque in the modern era, despite being the second-biggest economy in the world and a rising global power.

The picture is clearer than usual this time around, with the much-awaited twentieth Congress slated for an

October 16 opening. For quite some time, there has been a prevalent belief, both domestically and internationally, that the current General Secretary of the Communist Party of China, Xi Jinping, will defy contemporary convention and serve a third, five-year term. For years, Xi, who is also the president of the nation, has been pursuing this goal. For example, he drafted a constitutional amendment in 2018 that removed the president's term limits. His propaganda apparatus has enhanced the stature of Mao Zedong, who governed the People's Republic almost unopposed from its inception in 1949 until his passing in 1976. A compilation of his ideas called Xi Jinping Thought is required reading in Chinese schools. In the meantime, Deng Xiaoping, the leader who promoted a more group-oriented system of government, has received a lower priority in the official propaganda of the government. It is obvious that Xi has been preparing the way for his continued one-man rule over China's political structure.

Of course, it is impossible to predict with metaphysical certainty what will happen at the next Congress. As usual, the world will have to wait for the most recent major disclosure to find out if Xi is still in charge. In order to determine how much influence he will have in the upcoming years, it is perhaps more significant for the world community to learn who else will be sitting with him on the party's all-powerful Standing Committee of the Politburo. But unless something unexpected happens, world leaders should anticipate seeing Xi at the International Forum for a minimum of another five years.

Xi's continued hold on power has far-reaching consequences for China and the rest of the world. His choices in Beijing will have an impact not only on China but also on the world economy, technological advancement, international politics, and the nature of war and peace. Normally, at this point in China's political cycle, people around the world wonder: Who will rule China? The key query for this year is: What will Xi do with his influence?

3.7 The one-man rule is back.

It is crucial to comprehend how drastically Xi has changed Chinese governance in order to fully comprehend the significance of the twentieth Congress. The Communist Party promoted a system of collective leadership, which divided authority between the party and the state apparatus as well as within the party, starting in the 1980s. At congresses held every five years, this system was designed to include regular, peaceful handovers of power between leadership teams. Prominent figures held their positions for a maximum of ten years. The system was designed as a response to the unrest that marked the first thirty years of the People's Republic. Mao was more than just a dictator; in many ways, he was a Communist god, and everything he said was sacred. But for China, letting one individual have such tremendous power had disastrous results. Approximately 30 million Chinese people perished from starvation during Mao's Great Leap Forward (1958-1961), an ideologically driven attempt to use mass movements to propel a destitute China into the ranks of the rich. In 1966, he pursued a different course of action known as the Cultural Revolution, which led to ten years of widespread violence and economic paralysis. The campaign's goal was to remove the last remaining elements of an outdated, corrupt China and to strengthen Mao's political position. By the time Mao passed away in 1976, China was dangerously isolated, worn out, and impoverished.

The reformers, led by Deng Xiaoping, who was also a victim of the Cultural Revolution, eventually succeeded Mao and responded to the trauma of one-man rule. Deng stated, "Too much concentration of power is bad," in a speech on the topic in 1980. "It obstructs the socialist construction process, hinders the practice of socialist democracy and the democratic centralism of the Party, and keeps us from fully utilising collective wisdom." 2

Although there was still a lot of power held by the Communist Party—a terrible lesson from the 1989 Tiananmen Square massacre—there was more room within the party and the state for policy discussion. As a result, a broader spectrum of expertise was able to impact the policy-making process, and the Chinese state gained a reputation as a "technocracy"—a well-oiled, typically practical, and consistently predictable policymaking apparatus. One cannot divorce China's phenomenal economic achievements from the birth of this system of collective governance.

Xi has significantly changed this system. He has taken credit for other prominent members of the ruling class and marginalized them. For example, in the past, economic matters were the responsibility of the premier, who held the second-highest position in the ruling hierarchy. When Xi's leadership team first took over in 2012, Li Keqiang, the person currently holding that position, was almost universally expected to assume this responsibility. Li, however, has faded into the background under Xi. By controlling high-level commissions of top leaders on various policy areas and by elevating allies and loyalists into important positions within the party and state apparatus, Xi has taken control of the policymaking process across all sectors.

The constant promotion of Xi's personality cult has strengthened his hold on policy. The Chinese people (and the rest of the world, it seems) are shown by Xi as a bright theorist with the insight to bring the Chinese people back to life and find solutions to the trickiest issues confronting the global community. Xi's theories, which are summarised in Xi Jinping Thought, are similar to Mao's Little Red Book in that they have attracted inordinate attention and admiration. Just the sound of Xi's words can have bureaucrats and officials scrambling to interpret and carry out his directives.

Xi gets what Xi wants, for the most part. As a result, the choices and preferences of a single person have a greater and greater influence over Chinese policymaking. That has already made it harder to predict where Chinese policy will go.

As a result, predicting the direction of Chinese policy now involves figuring out Xi's priorities, whether they are personal, ideological, or national. Deng and his fellow reformers were, in a sense, precisely trying to avoid the kind of Chinese government that exists today. Once more, China and its enormous population have been left to fend for themselves at the whim of one person.

From a Christian perspective, the pursuit of justice and compassion, accountability, humility, and servant leadership are among the fundamental values and principles that underpin the need for change in government leadership. Long-term leadership can result in a concentration of power, a lack of accountability, and the repression of dissent—all of which are at odds with Christian principles. Leaders such as Xi Jinping and Vladimir Putin are prime examples of this.

It is critical to take these Christian principles into account when assessing the governance of any country, even though it is important to recognise that every country has a different political environment and that the people ultimately decide whether to change the leadership. By doing this, countries can make sure that their leaders respect the principles that advance justice and well-being for all of their citizens, particularly the most defenseless ones.

3.8 Islamic View like The Shura on Power Transfer with Refernce from the Qua'ran and Hadidth

The idea of shura, or consultation, is essential to Islamic governance and is used in both decision-making and leadership changes. Shura has its foundations in the Quran, and its principles are expounded upon in the Hadith, providing a thorough framework for comprehending the reasons behind the transfer of power in an Islamic setting. This essay will examine the Hadith and verses from the Quran that highlight the significance of Shura and how they add to our understanding of changing leadership in the context of Islam.

SHURA IN THE QUR'AN

The concept of shura is heavily stressed in the Quran, which serves as Islam's main source of guidance. A pivotal passage elucidating this notion can be discovered in Surah Ash-Shura (42:38): "And those who have responded to their Lord and established prayer and whose affairs are [determined by] consultation among themselves, and from what We have provided them, they spend." This verse makes a clear connection between the establishment of prayer and the response to Allah in the practice of shura.

The word "Shura" itself comes from a verse in Surah Ash-Shura in the Quran, emphasising how fundamental it is to Islamic law. It is stated that believers' consultation on issues of common concern is an essential component of their devotion to Allah.

Quranic Leadership and Accountability

The idea of leadership and the responsibility of those in positions of power are other topics covered in the Quran. "The Messenger has believed in what was revealed to him from his Lord, and [so have] the believers," says Surah Al-Baqarah (2:285). They have all professed faith in Allah, His angels, His writings, and His messengers, asserting that they do not distinguish between any of His messengers. "We hear, and we obey," they respond. We beg you, Lord, for forgiveness. The final destination is you."

This verse highlights the idea of obeying Allah and His messengers, implying that believers should heed the instructions given by divine revelation. The expectation that leaders uphold the values of justice and righteousness is implicit in this obedience. The community has a responsibility to address any deviations from these principles by means of consultation and appropriate action.

Hadith's Leaders' Accountability

The teachings of the Prophet Muhammad (peace be upon him) clarify the responsibility of leaders in more detail. According to one of Abu Bakr's hadiths, the Prophet exclaimed, "O people! They'll ask you about your leaders. You will question those in positions of authority about their subjects. A man will be questioned regarding his home."

The idea that leaders are subject to scrutiny and accountability is emphasized by this hadith. The Prophet's words highlight the significance of just and responsible leadership by implying that leaders will be questioned about their stewardship. The community can make sure that those in authority are carrying out their responsibilities in line with Islamic principles by holding leaders accountable.

Transitioning to Leadership and Practicing Shura

The Islamic framework's leadership transition process is a practical application of the principles of shura and accountability. Guidelines for these kinds of transitions are found in the Quran and Hadith, which guarantee that they follow the concepts of fairness and consultation.

Shura as a Tool for Changing Leadership

The Shura consultative process functions as a means of evaluating the leadership candidates and enacting changes as needed. The Prophet's companions held Shura in early Islamic history to choose a caliph following his death. This historical example emphasises how useful Shura is when there is a change in leadership.

Decisions made by Shura are not made at random but rather as a reflection of collective wisdom, thanks to its consultative nature. It promotes community cohesion and shared responsibility through discussion, consensus-building, and mutual consultation. The Quranic commandment to "conduct their affairs by mutual consultation" (Surah Ash-Shura, 42:38) is in accordance with this procedure.

Righteousness and Justice in Leadership Transitions

The importance that the Quran places on justice and righteousness in leadership is essential to comprehending the reasons behind the transfer of power. "Indeed, Allah commands you to render trusts to whom they are due and to judge between people with justice," according to Surah An-Nisa (4:58). That which you are instructed to do by Allah is excellent. Allah does, in fact, always hear and see."

This verse makes justice the cornerstone of good governance. A leadership transition must be seriously considered when officials stray from justice and betray the community's confidence in them. It is crucial to make sure that leaders behave in accordance with Islamic principles, and the community has a duty to address any deviation through legal means. This is highlighted by the Quranic injunction to judge with justice.

Unanimity in the Transition of Leadership

The Quran promotes seeking agreement when making decisions, particularly when it comes to leadership. "Therefore, by mercy from Allah [O Muhammad], you were lenient with them," says Surah Al-Imran (3:159). And they would have broken up about you if you had been harsh in heart and impolite [in speech]. Thus, forgive them, beg for your pardon, and confer with them about the situation. Once you've made up your mind, put your trust in Allah. Allah does, in fact, love those who rely on Him."

This verse emphasizes the Prophet's habit of conferring with his companions, highlighting the significance of group decision-making. Seeking agreement when it comes to leadership changes makes sure that everyone in the community is on the same page and reduces the likelihood of conflict.

Guidelines for Hadith Leadership Transitions

Hadith offers particular guidelines on the process of changing leadership in addition to the guidance found in the Quran. The Prophet said, "Whoever shows you the way to good, you should adopt it; and if he shows you the way to evil, it should not be adopted," according to a hadith recounted by Abu Huraira. This hadith emphasizes how the community has a duty to select leaders who will lead them in the direction of goodness and righteousness.

The significance of selecting a leader based on their piety and dedication to justice is emphasized by another Hadith that Abu Bakr recounts: "When people see an oppressor but do not prevent him from doing evil, it is likely that Allah will punish them all."

These hadiths support the idea that when the current leadership veers away from the path of justice and righteousness, a change in leadership is necessary and offer helpful guidance on assessing the traits and deeds of prospective leaders.

The Islamic perspective on the transfer of power is firmly based on the ideas of justice, righteousness, accountability, and shura. A thorough framework that stresses the consultative process of decision-making, the accountability of leaders, and the need for power transfers when leaders stray from the path of justice is offered by the Quran and Hadith. Early Islamic history's practical application of Shura, together with particular instructions from the Quran and Hadith, provides a model for ensuring that Islamic leadership transitions are carried out in a way that is prudent, just, and consistent with Islamic teachings. It is our responsibility as believers to maintain justice and righteousness in leadership, and the Quran and Hadith provide a framework for navigating this important facet of Islamic governance.

3.9 Islam's View of Government Leadership Rotation: A Comparative Study of China and Russia

Islam, one of the main religions in the world, has a special viewpoint on leadership and governance. It is a complicated and multidimensional question as to whether governments should change after every term. We seek to investigate the Islamic viewpoint on this matter in this lengthy discourse, employing Xi Jinping of China and Vladimir Putin of Russia as analytical points of reference. Even though these leaders might not govern according to Islamic principles, their lengthy reigns of power offer an important framework for considering Islamic perspectives on changing leadership.

The Islamic View of Governance

Prior to exploring the individual case studies, it is crucial to comprehend the Islamic viewpoint on leadership. Important insights can be gained from the Quran, the holy book of Islam, and the Hadith, which are the sayings and deeds of the Prophet Muhammad.

1. The Idea Behind Shura

The word "Shura," which means "consultation" or "deliberation," is one that the Quran promotes. Islamic governance is based on the fundamental principle of shura, which emphasises group decision-making. It is well known that the Prophet Muhammad himself sought advice from his companions. According to this idea, leadership should be participatory rather than authoritarian, allowing for changes in direction through discussion and agreement.

2. Responsibility

Another essential idea in Islamic governance is accountability. It is expected of leaders to answer to both God and the people they lead. According to the Quran, people in positions of authority will answer for their deeds. Therefore, those in positions of authority ought to answer to their constituents and be removed from office for misbehavior or poor management.

3. Equity and Justice

Islamic teachings place a strong emphasis on the value of justice and equity in government. It is the duty of leaders to govern in a just and equitable manner, guaranteeing that every citizen, regardless of background, has equal rights and legal protections. A leader's removal is considered justifiable if they do not follow these principles.

Putin and Russia's Vladimir

For more than twenty years, Vladimir Putin has been a significant figure in Russian politics. His several terms as Prime Minister and President have sparked debates regarding Russia's power structure and how it relates to Islam.

1. Dictatorial Rule

Putin's prolonged tenure in office and the concentration of power within the Kremlin give rise to worries about autocratic rule that goes against the Islamic concept of shura. The principle of Shura is undermined when power is concentrated in the hands of one person for a prolonged duration, thereby limiting the opportunities for consultation and collective decision-making.

2. Insufficient Accountability

Putin's administration has come under fire for being unaccountable. The Russian government's accountability has come under scrutiny due to the alleged manipulation of elections and the suppression of political opposition and media freedom. Islamic leaders ought to be held responsible for their deeds, and any kind of coercion or repression ought to be regarded as a violation of this precept.

Equity and Justice

Concern has been raised by reports of discrimination and violations of human rights against specific groups in Russia. Islamic thought places a strong emphasis on justice and fairness; discrimination of any kind and human rights violations are incompatible with these ideals.

Regarding Vladimir Putin's leadership in Russia, concerns are raised about whether his long-term tenure, lack of transparency, and perceived injustices in the political system are consistent with Islamic principles. There is a good case to be made from an Islamic standpoint for Russia to have new leaders.

3.10 China and Xi Jinping

With a concentration of power not seen in China since Mao Zedong's era, Xi Jinping has occupied a number of prominent positions. Under Xi's leadership, China's political environment has unique features that call for a closer look at Islamic values.

1. Concentration of Authority

China has seen a major concentration of power under Xi Jinping, which has reduced political pluralism and strengthened the Communist Party's hold on power. The Islamic concept of shura is not adhered to by this concentration of power since it restricts consultation and group decision-making.

2. Insufficient Accountability

Xi's administration in China has come under fire for lacking accountability and openness. Accountability issues have arisen because of the Chinese Communist Party's hold over the legal system and its suppression of political dissent. Islam holds leaders responsible for their deeds, and any lack of openness or repression of dissent is viewed as a transgression of this rule.

3. Rights Concerns for Humans

China's human rights record has come under international criticism, especially in light of the way it has treated Uighur Muslims and other minority groups. Concerns regarding justice and fairness have been raised by reports of forced labour, mass detentions, and persecution of religious groups. These claims contradict Islamic precepts, which place a strong emphasis on justice and equity in public administration.

From an Islamic standpoint, it is possible to argue that these factors—especially the concentration of power, the absence of accountability, and the concerns about human rights under Xi Jinping's rule—make a case for a change in China's leadership.

4. Islamic Law and Modern Administration

It is significant to remember that the Islamic viewpoint on governance and leadership is founded on timeless principles and is not restricted to any particular person or set of rules. The significance of justice, fairness, accountability, and group decision-making is emphasised by these principles. Islamic values can be applied to evaluate the legitimacy and efficacy of governance in any nation, including China and Russia.

Rotation and Term Limitations

Islamic principles stress the concepts of accountability and shura, which can be interpreted as supporting leadership rotation even though they do not specifically prescribe term limits for leaders. Since leaders are regularly held accountable for their actions, rotating leadership can offer chances for new perspectives and greater accountability.

What the Ummah Does

The Islamic view of governance heavily relies on the Ummah, or Muslim community worldwide. It is expected of the community to hold leaders responsible and make sure they follow Islamic law. The Ummah is obligated by moral and religious principles to pursue peaceful methods of bringing about change, including advocacy, protests, and elections, when necessary, when leaders depart from these ideals.

Difficulties with Implementation

It is critical to recognise that putting Islamic values into practice in modern governance can be challenging, particularly in nations with diverse political systems and populations. Scholars and religious authorities differ in their interpretations and debates regarding the application of these principles.

3.11 Argument in Favor of Regular Leadership Changes

There are strong arguments, grounded in Islamic principles, in favour of regular changes of leadership in both China and Russia. The ideals of justice, fairness, accountability, and shura are not being fully upheld in either nation, and a change in leadership may present a chance for their restoration.

1. Collective Decision-Making and Shura

Islamic thought places a great importance on group consultation and decision-making. The prolonged terms of office held by Vladimir Putin and Xi Jinping restrict the prospects for Shura and group decision-making since power is centralised around a single person or group. Reintroducing the idea of Shura at regular intervals of leadership transition can guarantee that a wider variety of opinions and viewpoints are taken into account during the decision-making process.

2. Responsibility

A fundamental component of Islamic governance is accountability. Because both Xi and Putin have been accused of rigging elections and repressing political dissent, there are concerns about accountability regarding their prolonged terms in office. Changing the leadership team on a regular basis can help to ensure transparency and oversight by holding leaders accountable for their actions.

3. Equity and Justice

Islamic beliefs emphasise the value of justice and

equity in the executive branch. Claims of discrimination, violations of human rights, and a lack of transparency have been made against both China and Russia. A leadership transition may present the chance to resolve these problems, reestablish confidence, and guarantee that justice and equity are maintained.

4. Transparent Leadership

In Islam, moral leadership is highly valued. It is expected of leaders to set a moral example for the people they represent. Changing leaders on a regular basis can help prevent leaders who have lost their moral integrity or who no longer uphold the standards of ethics that Muslims place on leaders from becoming entrenched.

3.12 Obstacles and Things to Think About

Although there is a compelling case from an Islamic standpoint for regular leadership changes, it is important to recognise the difficulties and factors that must be taken into account when putting such a model into practice in a variety of intricate political contexts.

1. Stability in Politics

Keeping the political system stable is one of the main priorities. If handled carelessly, frequent changes in leadership can cause political unrest, which can be harmful to the advancement and development of a nation. It's critical to strike a balance between stability and leadership rotation.

Election Procedures

The approach taken to change leadership is crucial. As is the case in many Western nations, democratic elections offer a peaceful and orderly way to change leadership. Finding a suitable way to replace leaders while respecting

Islamic principles can be difficult, though, in nations like China where the political system forbids direct elections.

3. Making Certain a Smooth Handoff

For political unrest to be avoided, a peaceful transfer of power is necessary. A peaceful transition of power can be facilitated and power vacuums can be avoided with the help of appropriate constitutional mechanisms and a dedication to the rule of law.

4. Relations Internationales

It is important to take into account the geopolitical ramifications of changing leadership, especially in nations like China and Russia that have substantial worldwide influence. A sudden change in leadership can have a significant impact on regional stability and international relations.

The Islamic view of governance, which is based on the concepts of justice, equity, responsibility, and shura, offers a framework for assessing the legitimacy and efficacy of leadership in any situation. Concerns have been raised regarding whether the long-term policies of Xi Jinping and Vladimir Putin in China and Russia are consistent with these ideals.

There is a good case to be made from an Islamic perspective for regular succession. These adjustments have the potential to restore the values of justice, fairness, accountability, and shura—values that might have been weakened by long-term rule. Putting this model into reality is difficult, though, and calls for giving careful thought to electoral processes, political stability, and the necessity of orderly handoffs between leaders.

Ultimately, the way that Islam views leadership serves as a reminder of the fundamental ideas that ought to guide any society's governance. The pursuit of justice, fairness, accountability, and group decision-making ought to be at the centre of leadership and governance objectives, whether in China, Russia, or any other country. Interpreting and putting these principles into practice in a way that is consistent with their particular contexts and values is the responsibility of the people, their leaders, and the global community.

3.13 Political Aspect of Islam with View on Power Transfer

The Quran, hadith literature, sunnah (accounts of the sayings and lifestyles attributed to the Islamic prophet Muhammad during his lifetime), Islam's history, and elements of political movements outside of Islam are the sources of political elements in Islam. Islam's traditional political ideas include the Caliphs (in Sunni Islam) and Imams (in Shia Islam), who are chosen or elected to lead as Muhammad's successors. They also emphasise the need for abiding by Islamic law (sharīfa), the obligation of rulers to seek input from their subjects (shūrā), and the significance of correcting oppressive rulers.

COMPATIBILITY WITH DEMOCRACY

General perspectives of Muslims

John Esposito and Natana J. DeLong Bas and two Western scholars identify four prominent attitudes among Muslims today regarding sharia and democracy: In [96]

- The promotion of democratic ideals, frequently coupled with the conviction that they are consistent with Islam, which can be publicly expressed in a democratic system, as demonstrated by the numerous demonstrators who participated in the Arab Spring upheavals;

- Support for democratic processes like elections coupled with moral or religious objections to parts of Western democracy that are deemed to be at odds with sharia, as demonstrated by Islamic scholars such as Yusuf al-Qaradawi;

- Opponents of radical Islamist movements and proponents of absolute monarchy reject democracy as a Western invention and support traditional Islamic institutions like shura (consultation) and ijma (consensus);

- A minority within the Muslim world maintains the belief that religion should be kept private in order to preserve democracy.

According to surveys by the Pew Research Centre and Gallup in nations with a majority of Muslims, the majority of Muslims do not see a conflict between democratic ideals and religious precepts. Instead, they prefer a political system in which sharia principles and democratic institutions can coexist. In

Political theories of Islam

Famous Muslim scholars who have worked to create contemporary, distinctively Islamic theories of socio-political organisation that adhere to Islamic law and values have developed three main perspectives on democracy, according to Muslih and Browers:

- Muhammad Rashid Rida, Sayyid Qutb, and Abul A'la Maududi developed the rejectionist Islamic perspective, which contrasts Islamic shura (consultation between ruler and ruler) with Western democracy and criticises copying of foreign ideas. This viewpoint, which emphasises the full application of sharia, was common among many movements aiming to create an Islamic state in the 1970s and 1980s, but its acceptance has declined in more recent times.

- The principles of maslaha (public interest), 'adl (justice), and shura are prioritised from a moderate Islamic perspective. If Islamic leaders uphold the public interest as defined by shura, then they are regarded as upholding justice. According to this perspective, shura serves as the foundation for representative government structures that resemble Western democracies but are more in line with Islamic than liberal Western values. Various versions of this viewpoint have been supported by Hasan al-Turabi, Rashid al-Ghannushi, and Yusuf al-Qaradawi.

Muhammad Abduh's emphasis on the role of reason in understanding religion has influenced the liberal Islamic perspective. It emphasises democratic values founded on intellectual freedom and pluralism. By referencing early Islamic texts, writers such as Fahmi Huwaidi and Tariq al-Bishri have created Islamic arguments in favour of granting non-Muslims full citizenship in an Islamic state. Others, such as Nasr Hamid Abu Zayd and Mohammed Arkoun, have used non-literalist approaches to textual interpretation to defend freedom and pluralism. A "religious democracy" founded on democratic, tolerant, and just religious thought has been advocated by

Abdolkarim Soroush. Liberal Muslims contend that religious understanding must be continually reexamined and that this can only happen in a democratic setting.

3.14 The Islamic Perspective on Democracy: Examining the Hadith and Quran with an Indian Case Study

The topic of democracy and its suitability for Islamic principles has been a subject of continuous discourse and analysis among the Muslim community. Using the Quran and Hadith as a guide, we will examine the general Islamic perspective on democracy in this investigation. We will also look at India as an example of a special situation where a sizable Muslim population lives under democratic principles. Using India as a case study, this analysis seeks to clarify the ways in which Islamic principles and democratic practice intersect.

Islamic Values and Democracy: A Quranic View

1. Consultation with Shuru:

The Quran highlights the importance of consultation, or shura, as a fundamental component of governance. According to Surah Ash-Shura (42:38), "And those who have responded to their Lord and established prayer and whose affairs are [determined by] consultation among themselves, and from what We have provided them, they spend." This verse supports democratic ideals that place a strong emphasis on participation by highlighting the value of group decision-making through consultation.

The idea of Shura establishes a basis for democratic values by emphasising the importance of community participation in decision-making.

2. Accountability and Justice:

The Quran emphasises the importance of accountability and justice in governance on numerous occasions. "Indeed, Allah commands you to render trusts to whom they are due, and when you judge between people, judge with justice," according to Surah An-Nisa (4:58). That which Allah commands you are excellent." In this verse, the significance of justice in decision-making—a cornerstone of democratic governance—is emphasized.

The Quran reinforces the idea of accountability by reminding leaders of their duty to act justly. "It will have [the consequence of] what [good] it has gained, and it will bear [the consequence of] what [evil] it has earned," says Surah Al-Baqarah (2:286). This idea supports democratic ideals, which hold leaders responsible for the people.

3. Consent and Freedom:

The Quran recognizes the existence of free will and personal preference. According to Surah Al-Baqarah (2:256), religion is free from coercion. The incorrect path has made the correct one obvious." This verse emphasises the value of individual freedom, which is a principle shared with democratic ideals, even though it primarily addresses matters of faith.

The verse in the Quran that addresses the appointment of leaders implies the idea of consent. The appointment of Adam as a vicegerent on Earth is related in Surah Al-Baqarah (2:30), suggesting some sort of divine approval and consultation. This idea is in line with democratic ideals, which place an emphasis on government that is established with the consent of the governed.

Hadith and Democracy:

1. Practice Consultation:

Examples from the Hadith provide additional support for the practice of shura. On a variety of topics, the Prophet Muhammad (peace be upon him) conferred with his companions. Notably, the Prophet asked his companions' opinions during the Battle of Uhud, demonstrating how Shura was put to use in real life.

The Prophet said, "O people!" in the Hadith that Abu Bakr recounted, emphasizing the responsibility of leaders. They'll ask you about your leaders. You will question those in positions of authority about their subjects. A man will be questioned regarding his home." This emphasises how leaders have a responsibility to the community, which is consistent with democratic ideals that hold leaders accountable to the people.

2. Justice and Equality:

The Prophet stressed justice and equality in his final sermon, which he gave while on his final pilgrimage. He said, "All mankind is from Adam and Eve; an Arab has no superiority over a non-Arab, nor does a non-Arab have any superiority over an Arab; also, a white has no superiority over a black, nor does a black have any superiority over a white, except by piety and good action."

This focus on justice and equality is consistent with democratic values, which place a high value on equal rights and opportunities for all people, regardless of their background.

3. Building Consensus:

The Hadith offers illustrations of how to reach a consensus when making decisions. According to the Hadith related by Abu Huraira, the Prophet advocated for reaching a consensus among his companions, saying that "whoever shows you the way to good, you should adopt it, and if he shows you the way to evil, it should not be adopted."

While reaching a consensus in the Hadith context differs from voting in a democracy, there are some parallels between the two processes in that decisions should be made collaboratively while taking the community's concerns and opinions into consideration.

3.15 A Case Study of India:

India is an exceptional case study because of its diverse religious and cultural landscape and the way a sizable Muslim population coexists with democracy there. Muslims and people of other religious backgrounds can participate in and be represented by the democratic ideals enshrined in the Indian Constitution.

1. Participation in Politics:

Muslims in India actively engage in civic society, vote, and are represented in politics as part of the democratic process. A wide variety of political parties, some of which explicitly represent the interests of the Muslim community, are permitted by the electoral system.

The political landscape clearly demonstrates the Shura principle, as political parties routinely engage in talks, coalition building, and consultations to establish governments at the federal and state levels.

2. The Legal Structure:

India's legal system, which consists of both civil and religious laws, takes into account the various religious practices that its people—including Muslims—follow. Within the parameters of the constitution, the democratic governance framework offers a forum for addressing the needs and concerns of diverse religious communities.

The Indian legal system, where people can seek justice through the courts regardless of their religious affiliation, is a manifestation of the Quran's emphasis on justice and accountability.

3. Diversity of Culture:

The Islamic values of justice and equality are consistent with India's secular culture and cultural pluralism. The coexistence of various cultures, languages, and customs shows a dedication to building an inclusive society.

The Indian democratic model preserves the values of justice, consultation, and individual freedom, even though it may not be an exact match for Islamic governance. This allows Muslims to freely practice their faith within a democratic framework.

3.16 Difficulties and Rebuttals:

1. Islamic versus secular governance:

The conflict between India's secular government and Islamic governance principles is one issue. Some contend that the Islamic conception of governance, which frequently incorporates religious ideas into political and legal frameworks, may not be entirely compatible with a secular state.

Opponents argue that a secular state might fail to sufficiently attend to the special religious and cultural requirements of the Muslim community, which could cause them to feel marginalized.

2. Political Engagement and Representation:

Despite political engagement, there are issues with Muslims' representation in elected offices. There are those who contend that the political representation of Muslims may not be commensurate with their population, raising concerns about the efficacy of democratic processes in accurately representing the diversity of the country.

Problems like educational opportunities and socioeconomic inequality may have an effect on how politically active and represented the Muslim community is.

The Quran and Hadith provide the general Islamic perspective on democracy. highlights values like Shura, accountability, justice, freedom, and consent. An intriguing lens through which to look at how Islamic principles and democratic governance intersect is the case study of India. Muslims can actively engage in a democratic system that allows for religious freedom and cultural pluralism, as the Indian context demonstrates.

Notwithstanding, certain obstacles persist, specifically pertaining to the conflict between secularism and Islamic governance, along with inquiries regarding sufficient representation. It is crucial to understand that there are numerous ways in which Islam and democracy can coexist, the Indian model being just one of them. The debate over whether Islamic principles are compatible with democratic governance is dynamic and ever-evolving, with various communities and regions interpreting these principles in light of their own particular political, cultural, and historical contexts. The continuous discourse between democratic norms and Islamic principles is essential to promoting inclusive governance that values the diversity of its people, irrespective of their religious affiliations.

3.17 A Jewish View of Governance Transition: Analysing Putin and Xi Jinping's Positions in China and Russia

The necessity and topic of government change are perennial debates in the fields of political science and international affairs. This debate has its roots in millennia of history, tradition, and the experiences of Jewish communities worldwide, according to the Jewish perspective. As a starting point, we will look at two well-known international leaders: Xi Jinping of China and Vladimir Putin of Russia, to better understand the Jewish perspective on the need for regular government changes. The extended rule of Putin in Russia and the consolidation of power under Xi in China provide important insights into the implications of long-term leadership and how they either align with or deviate from Jewish principles.

The Governmental Shift and Jewish Tradition

Jewish tradition and governance have a deep and intricate relationship. Jews have lived under many types of government since the time of the Bible, including monarchy, foreign occupation, and diaspora communities. The Jewish perspective on governance, including the need for change, has been shaped by this varied history. The following tenets of Jewish history and philosophy serve as a basis for comprehending why a change of government may be deemed necessary:

1. The narrative of the Israelites' Exodus from Egypt depicts Pharaoh as a despotic leader who oppressed them with an iron grip. This story establishes the basis for Jewish cynicism towards repressive and immutable political systems. The Exodus is celebrated on Passover, which serves as a powerful reminder of the significance of toppling unjust laws.

2. The cyclical structure of government in the Bible: The stories found in the books of Judges and Kings, in particular, illustrate a cyclical pattern of leadership. Israel is thought to alternate between righteous and immoral rulers on a constant basis, implying the necessity of regular change to bring justice and righteousness back.

3. Talmudic perspectives on governance: The Talmud, a foundational work of Rabbinic Judaism, addresses the interaction between the Jewish people and the state. It stresses the need to abide by the law, but it also suggests that when a ruler turns oppressive or unfair, a new leader may be required.

The Jewish perspective on government change is complex, focusing on the values of justice, righteousness, and resistance to oppression in light of this historical and theological context. We will analyse the terms of office of

Xi Jinping in China and Vladimir Putin in Russia against this background.

Vladimir Putin: The Long-Serving Leader of Russia

The reign of Vladimir Putin in Russia serves as a symbol of the difficulties that come with long-term leadership. Putin had been in power for more than 20 years, holding the dual roles of Prime Minister and President, as of my most recent knowledge update in September 2021. Allegations of electoral manipulation, the repression of political opposition, and the consolidation of power have all been characteristics of his rule. Regarding the values of justice, morality, and resistance to oppression, Jews are concerned about Putin's prolonged reign.

1. Justice and the rule of law: There have been claims of violations of human rights in Putin's Russia, including the repression of free speech, the persecution of political dissidents, and restrictions on the independence of the judiciary. Jewish tradition places a high value on the rule of law and justice, both of which can be compromised by long-term political power concentrations.

2. Leadership and righteousness: In Jewish thought, the idea of righteousness is central, and leaders are obliged to maintain high moral and ethical standards. Leadership morality becomes a question in a political climate rife with charges of authoritarianism and corruption.

3. Jewish history is replete with instances of people standing up against oppression, such as the Maccabees' uprising against the Seleucid Empire and the Jewish resistance movement during the Holocaust. Jewish concerns are raised when a single leader rules for an

extended period of time and creates an atmosphere where opposition is repressed.

Though not specific to the Jewish viewpoint, these issues are in line with Jewish ideals and experiences. Jewish communities and academics continue to debate and discuss whether Putin's extended rule is consistent with Jewish principles of governance.

Xi Jinping: China's Centralization of Power

The leadership of Xi Jinping in China offers an alternative, yet no less significant, case study. By the time I updated my knowledge in September 2021, Xi had eliminated term limits and established himself as the most powerful Chinese leader since Mao Zedong. He had also consolidated his power in previously unheard-of ways. Even in non-democratic settings like China, his leadership calls into question the necessity of reversing governments on a regular basis.

1. Centralization of power: Xi's efforts to consolidate power have sparked worries about the concentration of power in one person. Authoritarian leadership has always been frowned upon in Jewish tradition, particularly when it can result in oppression and the weakening of democratic checks and balances.

2. The function of checks and balances: Jewish political philosophy frequently emphasises the importance of these systems, which can take the form of democratic political systems or the advisors to a monarch. It becomes more difficult to stop abuses of power when authority is highly centralised.

3. Lessons from history: Jews have long lived under a variety of regimes, including monarchies, empires, and democracies. Lessons about the possible repercussions of extended, uncontested leadership have been learned from this history.

Even though China's political structure is very different from that of Western democracies, the Jewish perspective on governance raises issues with potential authoritarianism and power concentration. These issues can be examined through the prism of the Xi Jinping case.

3.18 Reforming Government: A Jewish Necessity

Jewish tradition and history make a compelling case for alternating governments on a regular basis, particularly when the ruling class grows ingrained and unaccountable. The biblical cyclical nature of leadership, the story of the Exodus, and the Talmudic perspectives on government all imply that in order to preserve the values of justice, righteousness, and resistance to oppression, change may be required.

It is noteworthy that this viewpoint is not exclusive to the Jewish community. Term limits and regular handovers of power are supported by a large number of political theorists and philosophers, irrespective of their backgrounds, in order to preserve robust democracies and guard against abuses of power. But the Jewish tradition gives this discussion a special moral and historical perspective.

Across national, religious, and cultural divides, the issue of government change and its necessity is a global one.

Jewish values such as justice, righteousness, and resistance to oppression are used as a prism to evaluate the terms of office held by leaders such as Xi Jinping and Vladimir Putin. Despite the fact that China's and Russia's political structures are very different from those of Western democracies, Jewish beliefs and experiences are shared in the worries about extended leadership and the concentration of power.

In the end, the Jewish viewpoint on governmental reform emphasises how crucial it is to preserve an accountable, just, and morally sound system of governance. A safeguard against the consolidation of power and the deterioration of democratic principles is the principle of change, whether it be through term limits, periodic elections, or other mechanisms. This viewpoint emphasises the significance of continual discussion and examination of leadership tenures, both in democratic and non-democratic contexts, to guarantee that the values of justice and righteousness are respected, even though it does not offer any particular policy recommendations.

3.19 Hinduism View

Hinduism is a sophisticated, multidimensional religion with a long history of philosophy. Its fundamental principles do not call for the adoption of a particular political structure or the regular alteration of the government. Still, there are aspects of Hindu philosophy that one could read to justify the notion of a shift in the system of government. This essay will examine these issues and highlight the possible drawbacks of long-term leadership by drawing comparisons between the periods of Xi Jinping's China and Vladimir Putin's Russia.

1. Religion and Time Cycles in Hinduism:

The idea that time and life are cyclical is deeply ingrained in Hinduism. The idea of "samsara," or the cycle of birth, death, and rebirth, embodies this fundamental idea of the religion. Hindu cosmology holds that the universe goes through cycles of creation, preservation, and destruction called "yugas." These yugas are believed to have different qualities and lengths, with the Kali Yuga, which is currently in effect, being regarded as the age of darkness and degeneration. The concept of cyclical time also suggests a shift in governance and a natural progression.

According to this cyclical theory of time, governments ought to alter on a regular basis in order to correspond with the shifting cosmic energies. Hinduism does not specify the length of time or frequency of these shifts, but the fundamental idea is that leaders should adjust to the demands and difficulties of the moment. The long terms of leaders such as Xi Jinping in China and Vladimir Putin in Russia serve as excellent examples of this idea.

2. Extended Guidance and Putin's Russia:

The longevity of Vladimir Putin's leadership in Russia is noteworthy. Since taking office as president in 1999, Putin has continued to exert influence in a number of capacities. Concerns concerning Russian political pluralism and democratic accountability have been raised by this prolonged tenure of power.

Some people view Putin's time as a symbol of the dangers of long-term leadership. A lack of political turnover can result in a concentration of power in the hands of one person or a small group, undermining the concepts of democracy and checks and balances, according to political scientists and academics. Hinduism's view of shifting leadership to accommodate cosmic cycles raises the possibility that a leader like Putin, who has held onto power for such a long time, is out of step with the times.

In addition, accusations of electoral irregularities and a crackdown on political dissent have been made against Putin's Russia. This brings to light another potential danger of long-term leadership: the abuse of power to stifle criticism and consolidate authority, undermining democratic norms and values.

These problems can be understood as a departure from the idea of "dharma" or righteousness in the context of Hindu philosophy, since those in positions of authority who refuse to give in to pressure to change may be perceived as acting against the laws of nature.

3. Extended Guidance and China under Xi Jinping

An additional example of prolonged governance in the modern era is the leadership of Xi Jinping in China. Since 2012, Xi has held the positions of President, Chairman of the Central Military Commission, and General Secretary of the Communist Party. His rise to power has sparked worries about China's lack of political diversity, freedom of speech, and human rights.

Under Xi's direction, the Chinese government has come under fire for its information censorship, information control, and handling of ethnic minorities like the

Uighurs. International condemnation of these actions and calls for responsibility have been made.

Hindus may view Xi Jinping or any other leader who holds onto power for an extended period of time as being out of step with the natural order of change and adaptation. Hinduism places a high value on moral obligation, or "dharma," and expects its leaders to rule with this in mind. Long-term leadership without regular adjustments runs the risk of straying from this moral obligation because leaders may grow less receptive to the changing needs of both the world and their constituents.

4. Philosophical Arguments in Support of Change:

As a multifaceted and pluralistic religion, Hinduism incorporates many different philosophical traditions and schools of thought. Over time, some of these traditions may offer philosophical explanations for changes in the administration.

Karma and Morality:

The idea of "karma" is essential to Hinduism. Karma is the term used to describe the moral and ethical fallout from one's deeds. Karma has an impact on the cycle of birth and rebirth, which is fundamental to Hinduism. A ruler who upholds wisdom and righteousness (in line with "dharma") builds up good karma and benefits the community. However, a leader may accrue bad karma and face consequences for themselves as well as their society if they become despotic, dishonest, or cling to power for an excessive amount of time.

According to this viewpoint, regular government transitions serve as a safeguard against leaders building up bad luck by holding onto office for too long. Periodic changes in leadership give rise to new leaders who may have a renewed commitment to dharma and are in line with the cyclical nature of time.

The Yugas Concept:

Hindu cosmology, as previously stated, separates time into yugas, each with distinct traits. The current era, known as the Kali Yuga, is distinguished by a fall in moral principles, discernment, and righteousness. In order to combat the negative trends, leaders in this day and age are expected to govern with extra caution and adherence to dharma.

Government change proponents contend that leaders who hold office for extended periods of time may not be able to adjust to the demands of a changing political landscape. It might not be appropriate for a leader who emerged in a more moral yuga to lead in a less moral one. Hence, it is possible to see recurring shifts in leadership as a means of bringing leadership into line with the traits of the dominant yuga.

Arguments Against Periodic Government Change:

It is important to recognize that there are those who argue against the idea of regular government changes based on Hindu principles. There are those who contend that this method oversimplifies the intricate structure of politics and government. The following are some refutations:

Continuity and Stability:

The stability and continuity that come with extended leadership are two of its main benefits. A long-serving leader can frequently offer stability during an uncertain period. Regular leadership turnover can impede long-term planning and cause political instability. The case for recurring government change may be contested by those who contend that stability and adaptability must coexist in harmony.

Leading Capability:

The case for regular government turnover is predicated on the idea that new administrators will always be superior to their forebears. This isn't always the case, though. Frequent changes in leadership could put less capable or experienced leaders in charge, which could result in bad governance.

Democratic Methods:

Regular elections determine the tenure of leaders chosen by the people in democratic societies. The democratic process is designed to include periodic transitions in leadership, which guarantee that elected officials answer to the people. Promoting further reforms outside of the current electoral cycle could jeopardise the democratic values that support these kinds of arrangements.

Hinduism can offer a philosophical foundation for arguing in favour of recurring political changes because of its cyclical conception of time and emphasis on dharma and karma. Leaders such as Xi Jinping in China and Vladimir Putin in Russia represent modern instances o

extended periods of leadership that have been criticised and raised issues with human rights, political plurality, and democratic accountability.

Though there are benefits to the argument for recurring changes in government based on Hindu principles, there are also drawbacks, as some may consider it to be an oversimplification of the difficulties involved in politics and governance. Any conversation of this kind must take into account the importance of maintaining democratic procedures, guaranteeing the calibre of leadership, and finding a balance between stability and flexibility.

Like many philosophical concepts, the idea of government change in Hinduism is ultimately interpreted differently depending on the political and cultural context. It serves as a reminder of how crucial it is to adjust to the shifting demands of society and guarantee that those in positions of power uphold the values of dharma and righteousness in their governance.

Chapter Four

Power Transition Perspective in India; a Case Study of Narendra Modi

4.1 The Decline Of India's Democratic System

India stands out as a prime illustration of the worldwide decline in democratic practises. India's democracy, despite initial scepticism, has defied numerous critics by exhibiting increased stability during its initial seventy years of existence. The process of India's democratic deepening can be observed through both formal and informal means. Formally, this has been achieved through the establishment of civilian control over the military and the sustained presence of vibrant multiparty competition over several decades. Informally, this progress is evident in the reinforcement of norms pertaining to the independence of the Electoral Commission, as well as the growing involvement of women and other social groups in the realm of formal political affairs.

India has experienced two notable instances of democratic decline: the period spanning 21 months from June 1975 to March 1977, commonly referred to as the Emergency, and a more recent decline that commenced with Narendra Modi's election in 2014. Under Prime Minister Modi's leadership, there has been a preservation of key democratic institutions in a formal sense. However, the fundamental principles and customary behaviours that uphold democracy have experienced a significant decline. The current democratic regression in present-day India presents a striking juxtaposition to the period of Emergency, during which Indira Gandhi systematically dismantled a significant portion of democratic institutions. This involved the suspension of elections, the detainment of political adversaries, the erosion of civil liberties, the suppression of independent media, and the enactment of three constitutional amendments that weakened the authority of the nation's judiciary.

However, according to democracy watchdogs, it is widely acknowledged that India currently occupies a position that lies in a grey area between a complete democracy and a complete autocracy. Various democracy-monitoring organisations employ different categorizations when classifying democracies. However, they unanimously classify India in the present day as a "hybrid regime," which denotes a political system that does not fully align with either a complete democracy or a complete autocracy. This phenomenon is novel. In the year 2021, Freedom House reclassified India's rating from Free to Partly Free, leaving only the category of Not Free as the remaining classification. In the aforementioned year, the Varieties of Democracy (V-Dem) project classified India as a "electoral autocracy" within its hierarchical framework encompassing closed autocracy, electoral autocracy, electoral democracy, and liberal democracy. The Economist Intelligence Unit has reclassified India as a "flawed democracy" on its scale that ranges from full democracy to flawed democracy, hybrid regime, and authoritarian regime. The democratic regression in India resulted in the reclassification of approximately 1.4 billion individuals, constituting a significant proportion of the global population of 8 billion, into the group of countries undergoing autocratization. The transition of India from a Free to Partly Free country has resulted in a significant reduction in the global population residing in Free countries. The absence of India within the ranks of democratic nations has had a notable impact on the overall population of our democratic world, regardless of how one delineates the boundaries between democratic, autocratic, and hybrid regions. The inquiry into the current state of democracy in India holds significant importance not only for the examination of the nation's political trajectory, but also for the broader comprehension of democratic patterns. India, currently the most populous country in the world, serves as the epicentre for the global struggle to uphold democratic principles.

There exists a divergence of opinion regarding the extent to which India has experienced a significant decline and transitioned into the realm of hybrid-regime classification. Predictably, the Indian government has responded by levelling allegations of Western prejudice, denouncing the characterization of India's democratic decline as "deceptive, inaccurate, and misguided." In August 2022, the Economic Advisory Council to the Prime Minister of India published a working paper highlighting discrepancies within democracy assessments. However, there exists a rationale for why evaluations of regimes, similar to the determination of interest rates by a central bank, are most effectively conducted by autonomous entities. It is worth mentioning that democracy monitoring organisations have been quite vocal in their assessment of the calibre of Western democracies.

However, there exists a small number of independent perspectives that challenge the reclassification of India as a hybrid regime. In the article titled "The Resilience of India's Democracy," Akhilish Pillamarri argues that the prevailing cultural and social trends observed in contemporary India should not be misconstrued as indicative of democratic regression. Instead, these trends reflect the existence of illiberal social norms within Indian society, particularly concerning freedom of speech, individual expression, and the acceptance of criticism. Consequently, the question arises as to whether India has truly deviated from the principles and practises of democracy. Furthermore, if indeed this is the case, can the transition of India into a hybrid regime be reversed? Affirmative responses can be provided to both inquiries.

4.2 What democracy means.

In order to assess the decline of democracy in India, it is imperative to establish a clear definition of democracy. This is essential for two reasons: firstly, it allows for a more informed analysis of the ongoing debate surrounding India's democratic regression, and secondly, democracy inherently implies a normative legitimacy that cannot be overlooked. Democracy is a political ideology that embodies a governance system characterised by its foundation in the principles of popular sovereignty, as famously articulated by Abraham Lincoln as being "of the people, by the people, and for the people." An examination of the non-normative aspects of democracy that serve as practical manifestations of this concept directs our attention to the criteria that can be employed in evaluating the condition of democracy in India.

The consensus among scholars is that there are five key institutions that are fundamental to the classification of a country as democratic. Among these five institutions, the primary and paramount processes are the elections held for the chief executive and legislature. Therefore, an essential component of democracy is the existence of authentic political competition. Countries in which individuals possess the right to participate in electoral processes, yet incumbents employ tactics that impede the opposition's ability to mobilise, are typically not classified as democratic nations. In addition to its other essential components, democracy necessitates the presence of governmental autonomy from external influences, such as colonial powers or influential military elites, which have the potential to impede or completely undermine democratic electoral processes. This autonomy serves as the third fundamental institutional element of democracy.

In addition to the aforementioned components, there are two other institutions that hold significant conceptual importance in a democratic system. These institutions, namely civil liberties (both de jure and de facto) and executive checks, serve as essential mechanisms for both citizens and independent branches of government to assess the performance of the governing body. Civil liberties, often referred to as the fourth pillar, encompass a range of rights and freedoms that safeguard individual autonomy and protect against government encroachment. On the other hand, executive checks, commonly known as the fifth pillar, involve mechanisms and processes that ensure accountability and oversight of the executive branch's actions and decisions. Together, these institutions play a vital role in upholding democratic principles and facilitating the evaluation of governmental performance. Numerous esteemed academics have aptly contended that definitions of democracy lacking the incorporation of fundamental civil liberties are insufficient. It is widely recognised that an autonomous press, facilitating the cultivation of discerning public sentiment, is an integral component of this pillar of civil liberties. The ultimate institutional component of democracy, executive checks, serves as a safeguard against an elected leader proclaiming "l'état, c'est moi." Democracy encompasses a collection of institutional frameworks that facilitate the establishment of a system of governance characterised by the principle of government accountability. There are two distinct forms of accountability that exist within a political system. The first is vertical accountability, which involves the relationship between the general population and the highest levels of elected government. This form of accountability is typically upheld through mechanisms such as elections and the presence of alternative political forces. The second form is horizontal accountability, which pertains to the checks and balances between the executive branch and independent institutions. These institutions, such as independent legislatures and courts, serve to constrain an elected executive from infringing upon civil liberties.

There are two significant implications that arise from this conceptualization of democracy with five pillars, which are relevant to our evaluation of India's current decline in democracy. One notable observation is that the scholarly understanding of democracy has appropriately broadened over the course of its development. Over the last 50 years, there has been a notable trend among authoritarian leaders to outwardly embrace democratic principles while simultaneously suppressing the very institutions necessary for its proper functioning. In response, democracy watchdogs have intelligently adjusted their approach by aiming to more effectively evaluate the presence of accountability within government institutions and the extent to which institutional rights are upheld not only in theory but also in practise.

An area of notable scholarly advancement in the realm of democracy is the recognition of the significance of institutional norms in reinforcing democratic systems. As articulated by Nancy Bermeo in her publication in 2016, the current era is marked by a phenomenon known as democratic backsliding, wherein the overt collapse of democratic systems is diminishing. Coup d'états are increasingly being substituted by promissory coups, wherein the removal of an elected government is justified as a means to uphold democratic legality. Similarly, executive coups are being supplanted by executive aggrandisement, whereby elected executives gradually diminish the checks on their own power through a series of institutional modifications that impede opposition forces from effectively challenging their preferences. Furthermore, election-day vote fraud is being substituted by preelection strategic manipulation, encompassing a variety of actions aimed at tilting the electoral landscape in favour of incumbents. In essence, the phenomenon of democratic decline can be characterised as a gradual erosion of democratic institutions, whereby troubled democracies are more prone to gradual deterioration rather than sudden collapse.

One of the most prominent indications of democratic erosion is observed when elected officials cast doubt on the legitimacy of any opposing factions and employ all legally permissible means to weaken their influence. In their scholarly work, Steven Levitsky and Daniel Ziblatt assert that by examining a diverse array of historical instances, it becomes evident that the establishment and adherence to unspoken regulations and societal expectations regarding the treatment of political adversaries play a pivotal role in safeguarding democratic systems from decline. The authors contend that the two primary norms of significance are opposition tolerance, which entails treating political adversaries as rivals rather than enemies, and forbearance, which involves the restrained utilisation of legal mechanisms to overcome opposition, such as executive orders, vetoes, and filibusters. The process of transitioning from contemporary democratic systems to autocracies is typically not an abrupt overnight occurrence. In democratic systems, the decline of democratic principles occurs gradually when the absence of tolerance towards opposition becomes prevalent, and elected officials employ legal mechanisms to suppress political dissent instead of seeking constructive resolutions through compromise.

The decline of democracy in contemporary India serves as a prime example of the significant erosion of norms that support democratic systems. The formal institutions of democracy in India, as assessed by Freedom House's political-rights category, which encompasses elections, competition, and autonomy, have exhibited a notable degree of stability during the past ten years. India's ranking in terms of civil liberties has experienced a consistent decline over the years, starting from 2019. This decline is evident in the decrease of its score from 42 out of a total of 60 points in 2010 to 33 points in 2023. The transition of India from the democratic category, which typically encompasses countries with scores above 70 on Freedom House's civil-liberties index, to the realm of a hybrid regime, typically characterised by scores ranging between 35 and 70, can be attributed to a decline of nine points in the aforementioned index. Furthermore, as elaborated upon in the subsequent analysis, the decision to downgrade is justified.

Another point of relevance is that a given regime has the potential to transition into autocracy through distinct mechanisms at various junctures. Various political systems can exhibit equal levels of undemocratic characteristics, albeit for distinct underlying causes. Democratic recessions do not necessarily have to manifest in a sensational manner, such as through military coups or the type of autogolpe, as observed during India's Emergency period under the leadership of Indira Gandhi. In the year 2023, Freedom House categorised both Iraq and Mali as nations lacking in freedom, assigning them identical scores of 29. However, it is important to note that these countries received such classification due to distinct and contrasting factors. Mali's political rights are assessed to be relatively low, with a score of 8 out of 40, primarily due to the absence of regular elections following successive military coups. Mali's position as a prominent full autocracy in terms of civil liberties is notable, as it ranks 21st out of a total of 60 possible points. This can be attributed to the relatively independent media landscape in the country, as well as the extensive rights granted to its citizens for expressing dissenting opinions and enjoying freedom of speech. In contrast, Iraq exhibits a relatively elevated level of political rights compared to other full autocracies, as evidenced by its score of 16 out of a total of 40 possible points. This is primarily attributed to the country's practise of conducting periodic and competitive elections, as well as its commitment to ensuring representation of diverse religious and ethnic factions within its political framework. However, Iraq's performance in terms of civil liberties is relatively low, scoring 13 out of a possible 60 points. This is primarily due to the frequent occurrence of documented cases where militias restrict the liberties of both citizens and journalists. Countries have the potential to fall below the democratic threshold when they experience a significant decline in certain areas. However, it is possible for countries to exhibit characteristics of hybrid regimes by experiencing a partial decline across various indicators, and this is precisely the situation observed in present-day India.

The concept of stable rights and declining liberties refers to the notion that while certain fundamental rights may remain relatively unchanged over time, the overall extent of individual liberties within a society may be diminishing.

The quality of India's democracy has historically been suboptimal. The formal practise of independent and competitive elections, accompanied by a wide array of civil liberties, although resulting in a significant poverty reduction initiative and the implementation of the world's most extensive affirmative-action programme, was not without its limitations. However, democracy also possessed an inherent mechanism for self-correction, enabling the removal of incumbents from positions of power. The autocorrect feature is currently at risk of becoming endangered, primarily due to its prevalent usage in informal contexts. India's average political-rights score, as measured by Freedom House, remained consistent in the nine years preceding Modi's assumption of power and the nine years following 2014. This score encompasses the pillars of elections, competition, and autonomy. The potential for a change in incumbency persists in electoral contexts, although it is highly unlikely. This is due to the significant erosion of the de facto safeguarding of civil liberties and executive constraints by the Modi government, which are considered fundamental pillars of democracy. The decline of India's contemporary democracy can be attributed to the decrease in its civil-liberties rating.

The legal entitlement to express dissent, which has historically been inconsistently safeguarded in Indian courts, continues to exist in a legal sense. However, the practical feasibility of engaging in vocal dissent without facing pervasive harassment has effectively diminished. Prior to the ascension of the Bharatiya Janata Party (BJP) government in 2014, it is worth noting that India's media landscape, although predominantly dynamic and unrestricted, occasionally experienced instances of censorship. In contemporary times, although the media retains its legal freedom to express dissenting views, the prevalence of harassment towards independent journalism and the consolidation of ownership structures have resulted in journalists and individuals exercising a significant level of self-restraint in their reporting. The existing mechanisms to oversee executive power are experiencing a notable decline in their effectiveness.

Civil liberties that are severely limited or restricted. Since the year 2016, there has been a notable curtailment of civil liberties, both within the bounds of the law to a certain degree, and more significantly in practical terms. According to CIVICUS, a global organisation dedicated to monitoring civil liberties across 197 countries, India is currently categorised as "repressed" on its scale measuring the decline of open, narrowed, obstructed, repressed, and closed conditions. The demotion from the "obstructed" status, which occurred in 2019, signifies that India's civic space is characterised by the potential for civil society members who voice criticism against those in power to face various forms of oppression, including surveillance, harassment, intimidation, imprisonment, injury, and even death, as stated on the organization's website. In terms of comparative ratings among neighbouring countries, India now shares the same classification as Pakistan and

Bangladesh, while being placed in a lower category than Nepal and Sri Lanka.

The utilisation of colonial-era sedition laws and the Unlawful Activities Prevention Act (UAPA) has become more prevalent within the Modi government as a means to suppress dissenting voices. The authorities have consistently employed sedition laws to apprehend individuals who express dissent through various means such as posters, social media posts, slogans, personal communications, and, in a particular instance, by sharing celebratory messages in response to a victory by the Pakistani cricket team. There was a notable increase of 28 percent in sedition cases reported during the period spanning from 2010 to 2021. After the assumption of power by Prime Minister Modi in 2014, a significant majority of sedition cases, specifically 96 percent, were initiated against individuals who expressed criticism towards the government. According to a report, it has been estimated that within a span of one year, a total of ten thousand tribal activists residing in a specific district were subjected to charges of sedition due to their assertion of land rights.

In 2019, an amendment was made to the Unlawful Activities Prevention Act, granting the government the authority to designate individuals as terrorists, even in the absence of a direct affiliation with a terrorist organisation. The absence of a judicial redress mechanism renders it impossible to challenge this categorization. The current legislation explicitly designates its applicability to individuals engaged in any action deemed "likely to pose a threat" or "likely to instill fear in individuals." Notably, between the years 2015 and 2019, there was a notable surge of 72 percent in apprehensions made under the UAPA, wherein a staggering 98 percent of the arrested individuals were detained in custody without the provision of bail.

The increased utilisation of these reinforced legislations represents a substantive novelty and has had a profound inhibitory effect on the expression of dissent. The state has employed a strategy of intimidation against opposition by employing a broad categorization of criticisms of government policy as being in opposition to the national interest, commonly referred to as "anti-national." Additionally, the state has mobilised a significant number of volunteers to actively identify instances of dissent on online platforms that are deemed problematic. The term "anti-national" has been widely disseminated by politicians affiliated with the Bharatiya Janata Party (BJP), exhibiting a consistent tendency to direct it towards specific individuals, causes, and organisations. The initial focus of the targeting was on individuals within the academic community, including university administrators and faculty members, who were subjected to investigations, disciplinary actions, or forced resignations due to their perceived political beliefs. However, these strategies were rapidly expanded to encompass individuals who expressed prominent dissent.

The Muslim community in India, which accounts for approximately 14 percent of the total population, has experienced a significant decrease in civil liberties. Instances of anti-Muslim violence, such as lynchings or mob killings, have experienced a significant increase.

Based on data from IndiaSpend, there has been a significant increase in incidents of mob-lynching related to bovines, particularly involving rumours of individuals involved in beef handling, predominantly Muslims. These incidents have become a more prominent form of violence in India since 2010, with approximately 97 percent of bovine-related attacks occurring between 2010 and 2017 taking place after the assumption of power by Prime Minister Modi in 2014. It is widely believed that a significant proportion of individuals who have fallen victim to public acts of violence are affiliated with the Muslim faith. According to various independent international organisations, including Human Rights Watch and the United States, the largest minority in India currently resides in an extensive atmosphere characterised by fear. The Commission on Religious Freedom is a governmental body established to address matters related to the protection and promotion of religious freedom. The enactment of the Citizenship Amendment Act by Parliament in 2019 resulted in the institutionalisation of discriminatory practises against Muslims, as it explicitly excluded Muslim refugees from the expedited citizenship procedure. It is widely perceived by analysts that the aforementioned Act, in conjunction with the proposed establishment of a nationwide citizen registry, may potentially be employed in a coordinated manner to marginalise Muslim voters who are unable to furnish the necessary documentation to substantiate their citizenship status. The state of Jammu and Kashmir, which is the sole Muslim-majority region in India, is currently undergoing a curtailment of its civil liberties that bears striking resemblance to the period of India's Emergency. This similarity is evident in the classification of Indian Kashmir as "Not Free" by Freedom House.

The limitation of individual freedom to express dissent is further exacerbated by legal restrictions on the right to assemble. According to a report published in 2021 by the International Centre for Not-For-Profit Law, an evaluation of the state of freedom of assembly in India revealed a rising adoption of a punitive and security-oriented strategy. This approach has been accompanied by a noticeable inclination towards stigmatizing and criminalizing public demonstrations, which includes the disparagement of individuals responsible for organising such assemblies.

The government has consistently implemented restrictions on internet access, which serves as the primary medium for organizing protests. India is at the forefront of global internet shutdowns orchestrated by the government, having implemented 84 such shutdowns in 2022. These deliberate disruptions are commonly enforced prior to and during protests, aiming to hinder efficient public coordination. Notably, the criteria for suspending these shutdowns often lack clarity. The findings of the report indicate that although there has been a slight erosion in the legal safeguards for freedom of speech and assembly, there has been a substantial decline in the practical safeguards for these rights.

Civil society's critics of the government often face repeated instances of administrative harassment. In 2020, the Modi administration implemented stricter measures within the

Foreign Contribution Regulation Act (FCRA) with the aim of exerting control over civil society autonomy. These measures primarily focused on regulating the logistical aspects of foreign-fund transfers, imposing restrictions on the types of expenditures and the sharing of funds among non-governmental organisations (NGOs). Additionally, the amendments granted discretionary powers to both central and state governments to suspend NGOs and prohibited public servants from affiliating with such organisations. Government authorities have employed a methodical approach in utilising financial audits and conducting tax-related raids on various civil society groups, such as Amnesty International, Greenpeace, the Centre for Policy Research, the Ford Foundation, the Lawyers Collective, and Oxfam. These actions have been carried out based on technical justifications that adhere to legal frameworks.

In the past ten years, Indian media outlets have significantly limited their ability to criticise the government, primarily as a result of explicit intimidation tactics and structural modifications. Since 2014, India's position in the World Press Freedom Index, as determined by Reporters Without Borders, has declined to 161st out of 180 countries. This ranking places India below several nations including Afghanistan, Belarus, Hong Kong, Libya, Pakistan, and Turkey. As per the organization's findings, Indian journalists occasionally encounter death threats and are frequently subjected to social-media hate campaigns orchestrated by troll farms associated with the government. Major media networks perceive limitations in their ability to openly critique the government led by Prime Minister Modi. A comprehensive examination of prime-time television debates aired on the channel Times Now during a three-month period in 2020 revealed a notable absence of episodes wherein the Modi government was subjected to any form of criticism. An independent analysis conducted on RepublicTV's coverage from 2017 to 2020 revealed a consistent bias in favour of the Modi government and its policies. Additionally, it is noteworthy that Prime Minister Modi has refrained from engaging with the media through press conferences for the past nine years.

The erosion of media independence is exacerbated by various practises, including selective licencing, the acquisition of independent networks by businessmen associated with Modi, and the harassment faced by the remaining few independent outlets. In order to engage in television broadcasting, it is imperative for entities to obtain a licence from the government. Conversely, licences may be withheld from domestic organisations that are deemed critical or dissenting in nature. The licencing authority of the government delayed the issuance of a licence to Raghav Bahl, the founder of the news website Quint, who was collaborating with Bloomberg. This delay was of such significance that it led to the closure of the company's television division. In 2019, Bahl underwent an investigation and was subsequently charged with the offence of money laundering.

The presence of numerous news organisations in India may initially suggest a flourishing media landscape; however, a closer examination of the operational ownership structure reveals a different reality. According to the findings of the independent Media Ownership Monitor, there is a notable inclination towards consolidation and eventual dominance of content and public sentiment in India. Mukesh Ambani, a businessman who maintains strong connections with Modi, exercises direct control over media establishments that reach a substantial audience of at least 800 million Indian individuals. In December 2022, Gautam Adani, a prominent associate of Prime Minister Modi, acquired NDTV, India's final significant independent television network. As per analysts' assessment, the acquisition of NDTV by Adani signifies the culmination of independent media in India, resulting in the control of the country's major television news channels by billionaires with significant affiliations to the Indian government. Although a few smaller sources of independent news remain, they have encountered instances of tax raids and legal actions in response to their reporting activities since 2013.

The government also directs its attention towards international news organisations due to their critical stance, often framing negative foreign news coverage as a deliberate effort to hinder India's progress on the global stage. In February 2023, the Indian offices of the British Broadcasting Corporation (BBC) were subject to a raid, occurring shortly after the news organisation had aired a documentary that presented a critical perspective on the government led by Prime Minister Narendra Modi. Recently, the laws enacted during the Emergency period were employed to prohibit the dissemination of the BBC documentary and any related excerpts within the borders of India. During the occurrence of the raids, Gaurav Bhatia, the spokesperson for the Bharatiya Janata Party (BJP), made a statement referring to the British Broadcasting Corporation (BBC) as the "most corrupt organisation in the world." At Oxford University, a group of several Indian students, whom I am currently instructing, arranged a private screening of a documentary. It was evident that a sense of apprehension permeated among these students. The attendees were requested to abstain from engaging in social media activities and refraining from exchanging messages on the WhatsApp platform. This precautionary measure was implemented due to the existence of video evidence depicting law enforcement officials requesting individuals to unlock their mobile devices during routine encounters.

The erosion of horizontal accountability. The level of legislative oversight over executive actions has experienced a decline in substantive terms during the tenure of Prime Minister Modi. The committees of India's primary parliamentary bodies play a crucial role in overseeing the executive branch, conducting thorough evaluations and deliberations on the merits of all proposed legislation. During the period encompassing the 2009-2014 parliament, a significant proportion of bills, amounting to 71 percent, underwent thorough examination by committees. However, in the subsequent parliament from 2014-2019, during Prime Minister Modi's initial term, the scrutiny of bills by committees decreased substantially to only 25 percent. The level of scrutiny has experienced a decrease to 13 percent since the year 2019, and no legislative bills were referred to a committee throughout the duration of the 2020 pandemic. Several significant laws and political decisions in India in recent years, such as the implementation of a nationwide lockdown with only four hours' notice, demonetization, and the enactment of farm laws, were enacted without proper parliamentary consultation and despite opposition protests. The Modi administration has implemented a series of legal revisions aimed at diminishing the safeguards provided to whistleblowers.

The escalating absence of executive accountability to Parliament is further intensified by a progressively passive judiciary. The Supreme Court of India serves as the guardian of the nation's constitution and, consequently, safeguards civil liberties. In the period preceding 2014, there was a notable increase in the perceived independence of the Supreme Court, leading to its recognition as the "most powerful apex court in the world." However, there has been a significant shift in this perception, as the central government has controversially reassigning justices who displayed independent thinking and reducing the effectiveness of norms that served as checks on executive authority. The aforementioned actions led to an extraordinary press conference in 2018 by the four most senior members of India's Supreme Court, wherein they expressed concern that the chief justice's atypical allocation of cases might indicate political intervention. One of the aforementioned justices, namely Jasti Chelameswar, composed an open letter directed towards the chief justice, wherein he expressed disapproval regarding the amicable relationship between the Judiciary and the Government in any given state, as it poses a significant threat to the principles of democracy. It is noteworthy that the Supreme Court has consistently rendered rulings in favour of the Modi government on various significant political matters, including but not limited to the Ayodha temple dispute, the Aadhar biometric identification system, the application of habeas corpus in Kashmir, electoral bonds, and the Prevention of Money Laundering Act. This signifies a departure from previous circumstances. The discernible disparity between the Supreme Court during the period of Emergency and its present state is negligible. There are proponents who assert that in contemporary times, an Emergency can be perceived as being effectively "undeclared."

4.3 Possibility of preserving Indian democracy?

The current state of democracy in India, similar to other nations globally, is not presently experiencing a demise characterized by a military coup or the orchestrated detention of political adversaries. In recent times, authoritarian leaders have acquired the ability to employ democratic rhetoric while simultaneously implementing autocratic practises. This entails upholding a superficial appearance of democratic governance, while actively engaging in the suppression of opposition and restricting the scope for legitimate dissent. India's democratic institutions are currently facing challenges, as evidenced by the disqualification of Modi's political rivals from participating in elections. However, the main factors contributing to India's transition into a hybrid regime are the limited access of ordinary citizens to critical evaluations of government policies, the lack of freedom to express opinions and gather peacefully without fear of harassment, and the absence of effective checks on executive power.

While there is indeed evidence of a decline in India's democratic state, it is important to note that this decline is not necessarily permanent and can potentially be reversed. Hybrid regimes, despite their inherent stability, experience genuine instances of political accountability during elections, provided that the secrecy of ballots is maintained and the electoral process is adequately monitored. Even in the case of entirely autocratic regimes that have well-developed surveillance policies, there are instances where effective protests can occur. This is because the inherent structures of autocratic power hinder these regimes from obtaining a precise comprehension of the concerns expressed by their citizens, which is an area where democracies excel. The enduring potential of mass dissent has been underscored by recent protests targeting China's zero-covid strategy, Iran's morality police, and India's farm laws.

In order to facilitate the resurgence of democracy in India, it is imperative for a bona fide opposition party to emerge, one that possesses robust organisational foundations. The Indian National Congress was previously a political party that possessed strong grassroots linkages. However, in 1969, Indira Gandhi initiated a split within the party, resulting in the dissolution of its grassroots-party infrastructure, as she sought to consolidate power at the central level. The recent state assembly elections in Karnataka, a southern state known for housing India's Silicon Valley, have highlighted the ongoing electoral vulnerability of the Bharatiya Janata Party (BJP) and potentially can be attributed to the grassroots campaign led by Rahul Gandhi, known as Bharat Jodo Yatra. The success of the Congress party in these elections serves as evidence of the aforementioned vulnerability. The Aam Aadmi Party (AAP) has emerged as a promising political entity with the ability to expand its influence beyond the confines of Delhi, albeit on a relatively smaller scale. However, both political parties encounter a formidable challenge in their efforts to achieve sustained growth and progress beyond the influence of their charismatic leaders. In order to be effectively utilised, power must be organised in a manner that extends beyond the capabilities of individual actors. Challenging the Bharatiya Janata Party (BJP), an organisation with deep-rooted historical development spanning almost a century, will undoubtedly present significant difficulties. However, it is not an insurmountable task.

4.4 The history of Narendra Modi in the history of India's Politics

The tenure of Narendra Modi in the realm of Indian politics has been characterised by noteworthy advancements and transformations. The individual initially gained recognition as the Chief Minister of Gujarat in 2001, subsequently holding this position for three terms. In the year 2014, he assumed the position of Prime Minister of India, spearheading the Bharatiya Janata Party (BJP) to achieve a momentous triumph in the nationwide elections. The following is a comprehensive account of the tenure of Prime Minister Narendra Modi's government in India.

Chief Minister of Gujarat from 2001 to 2014.

Narendra Modi assumed the position of Chief Minister of Gujarat in October 2001 subsequent to the occurrence of a seismic event that impacted the state. During his term as Chief Minister, there were notable instances of economic progress as well as instances of controversy.

The administration led by him received commendation for its efforts in fostering industrial expansion in the state of Gujarat, thereby earning him the epithet "Gujarat's Vikas Purush" (the individual responsible for Gujarat's development). The state witnessed substantial economic expansion during his period of leadership.

Nonetheless, the government under his leadership faced substantial criticism regarding its management of the 2002 Gujarat riots, resulting in the loss of more than a thousand lives, predominantly among the Muslim populace. Prime Minister Modi was confronted with accusations of inadequate measures taken to curb the outbreak of violence.

Despite the contentious nature of the riots, Narendra Modi maintained a significant level of popularity within the Bharatiya Janata Party (BJP) and was widely regarded as a resolute and charismatic figure.

Prime Minister of India from 2014 to the present:

In the year 2014, Narendra Modi successfully led the Bharatiya Janata Party (BJP) to a decisive triumph in the general elections, subsequently assuming the position of the 14th Prime Minister of India.

The Prime Minister's tenure has been characterised by a succession of ambitious initiatives, such as "Make in India," "Swachh Bharat Abhiyan" (Clean India campaign), "Digital India," and the "Pradhan Mantri Jan Dhan Yojana" (financial inclusion programme).

The implementation of the Goods and Services Tax (GST) in 2017 was the most significant and controversial reform during his tenure. Its primary objective was to streamline India's intricate tax system.

In 2016, Prime Minister Modi implemented a policy known as "Demonetization," which entailed the abrupt removal of high-value currency notes as a measure to address the issues of illicit funds and unethical practises. The outcome of this action was characterised by a combination of positive and negative outcomes, leading to a significant level of controversy and extensive discussions among scholars and experts.

In the year 2019, Narendra Modi successfully led the Bharatiya Janata Party (BJP) to achieve a significant triumph in the elections, thereby securing a subsequent term as the Prime Minister of India. The current election witnessed the party's expansion of its influence and the further consolidation of its political power.

Modi's foreign policy has been characterised by a heightened assertiveness in international affairs, aimed at bolstering diplomatic ties with nations such as the United States, Russia, and other global partners. Furthermore, he has been actively engaged in regional diplomacy within the South Asian context.

The government under his leadership has implemented a range of social welfare initiatives, such as the "Ayushman Bharat" health insurance scheme, the "Pradhan Mantri Awas Yojana" aimed at providing housing, and the "Ujjwala Yojana" which focuses on ensuring access to clean cooking fuel for households.

In terms of national security, the Modi administration has adopted a firm approach towards counterterrorism, specifically in the context of India's bilateral relations with Pakistan and the enduring matter of Kashmir.

3. Critiques and Disputes:

The handling of issues such as economic slowdown, unemployment, and the implementation of reforms by the Modi government has been subject to criticism from certain quarters.

Critics have raised apprehensions regarding the prevailing state of religious and social harmony in India, highlighting instances of religious violence and discriminatory practises targeting minority communities.

The management of the COVID-19 pandemic has also been a topic of critique, with apprehensions expressed regarding the adverse effects of the lockdown on marginalised communities and the healthcare system's ability to cope with the situation.

4. The Significance and Influence:

The tenure of Narendra Modi in the realm of Indian politics has had a profound and enduring influence on the nation. The individual's leadership approach is distinguished by a resolute decision-making process and a notable focus on fostering economic growth and promoting nationalistic ideals. The initiatives and policies implemented by his government have exerted a significant impact on both the domestic and international affairs of India.

As of the most recent update in January 2022, Narendra Modi's tenure as the Prime Minister of India remained in progress, with his legacy continuing to undergo development. It is important to acknowledge that subsequent advancements may have transpired subsequent to the aforementioned period, thus necessitating the consultation of current and reliable sources to obtain the most recent information pertaining to his administration and its influence on India.

4.5 The Controversial Use of Central Agencies in India: N. Modi's Government and Its Alleged Pressure on Political Opponents

In recent times, there has been a noticeable presence of apprehensions and disputes in the Indian political domain regarding the purported utilisation of central investigative bodies, namely the Central Bureau of Investigation (CBI) and the Directorate of Enforcement (ED), with the intention of exerting influence over political adversaries and stifling opposition. The allegations surrounding the Bharatiya Janata Party (BJP), under the leadership of Prime Minister Narendra Modi, have brought into question the impartiality and autonomy of these significant institutions. This article delves into the involvement of the Central Bureau of Investigation (CBI), Enforcement Directorate (ED), and other central agencies in the realm of Indian politics. It critically examines the allegations surrounding their potential exploitation for the purpose of targeting political opponents and suppressing dissenting voices within the opposition.

Understanding the Central Bureau of Investigation (CBI) and Directorate of Enforcement (ED)

Prior to exploring the controversies pertaining to the utilisation of central agencies, it is imperative to comprehend the roles and functions of the Central Bureau of Investigation (CBI) and the Enforcement Directorate (ED) within the governmental framework of India.

The Central Bureau of Investigation (CBI):

The Central Bureau of Investigation (CBI) is a governmental agency responsible for conducting investigations and maintaining law and order within the jurisdiction of the Indian government.

The Central Bureau of Investigation (CBI) is widely regarded as India's foremost investigative agency, having been originally established in 1941 under the name of the Special Police Establishment. The organisation functions within the purview of the Ministry of Personnel, Public Grievances, and Pensions, and is tasked with examining a diverse array of matters, encompassing corruption, economic transgressions, fraudulent activities, and prominent criminal instances. The Central Bureau of Investigation (CBI) assumes a pivotal role in the preservation of law and order, the facilitation of justice, and the preservation of the integrity of governmental institutions.

The Directorate of Enforcement (ED):

The Directorate of Enforcement (ED) is an authoritative body responsible for the enforcement and implementation of various laws and regulations.

The Enforcement Directorate (ED) is tasked with the enforcement of the provisions outlined in the Foreign Exchange Management Act (FEMA) and the Prevention of Money Laundering Act (PMLA) within the jurisdiction of India. The primary objective of the organisation is to address the issue of money laundering, conduct investigations into financial crimes, and enforce adherence to foreign exchange regulations. The jurisdiction of the ED encompasses matters pertaining to economic and financial infractions, particularly those involving cross-border transactions, and prioritises the safeguarding of the nation's economic stability.

Controversies Surrounding the Misuse of Central Agencies

Although the existence of these agencies is crucial for the preservation of law and order and the enforcement of legal principles, apprehensions have arisen regarding their potential for abuse in targeting political adversaries and stifling dissent. Numerous occurrences have prompted inquiries regarding the neutrality and autonomy of the Central Bureau of Investigation (CBI) and the Enforcement Directorate (ED), giving rise to accusations of political intervention. Several significant controversies and allegations have emerged, warranting attention and scrutiny.

1. Misuse of CBI for Political Vendettas:

One concern that arises is the potential for the misuse of the Central Bureau of Investigation (CBI) as a tool for political vendettas.

The Central Bureau of Investigation (CBI) has frequently encountered accusations of being utilised as a means to settle political scores with adversaries. One of the most prominent instances involved the Central Bureau of Investigation's (CBI) participation in the inquiry of the Ishrat Jahan encounter case, wherein the agency's conduct was subject to censure due to allegations of political party influence.

2. Targeting Opposition Leaders:

The focus of this inquiry pertains to the deliberate selection of opposition leaders as subjects of attention or actions.

The Modi administration has been accused by opposition leaders of employing the Central Bureau of Investigation (CBI) in a discriminatory manner to specifically target them. An illustrative instance pertains to the matter of P. Chidambaram, a former Finance Minister, who was confronted with allegations of engaging in money laundering and corruption. Critics contended that the aforementioned charges were driven by political motivations with the intention of suppressing a prominent voice of opposition.

3. The Controversy Surrounding Enforcement Directorate Raids

The Enforcement Directorate (ED) has undertaken notable operations targeting prominent figures from the opposition and business community, thereby giving rise to apprehensions regarding the agency's neutrality. There has been a widespread dissemination of allegations regarding the utilisation of these raids as a means to exert pressure on political adversaries, with critics contending that the government is endeavouring to stifle dissent.

4. Temporal Aspects of Investigations:

The timing of investigations and raids conducted by central agencies has been subject to scrutiny by critics, particularly in relation to their occurrence prior to elections or significant political occurrences. These actions have been perceived as deliberate efforts to undermine the credibility and standing of opposition leaders and political parties in anticipation of crucial electoral competitions.

5. Dilution of Federalism:

The concept of dilution of federalism refers to the weakening or reduction of the principles and powers associated with a federal system of government.

The purported misappropriation of central agencies also raises inquiries regarding the federal structure of India. State governments have asserted that the central government utilises these agencies as a means to erode the autonomy of state governments and meddle in political affairs at the state level.

4.6 Case Studies and Examples

The utilisation of case studies and examples is a prevalent approach in academic research and discourse. These tools serve to illustrate and support theoretical concepts, providing concrete instances that demonstrate the application and relevance of the discussed ideas.

In order to elucidate these contentious issues, let us delve into specific instances that have attracted considerable scrutiny:

1. The Controversy Surrounding Alok Verma:

In the year 2018, Alok Verma, who held the position of Director of the Central Bureau of Investigation (CBI) at the time, was compelled to take leave by the government led by Prime Minister Narendra Modi, in the midst of an internal conflict for authority within the agency. The aforementioned action received criticism due to its perceived political motivations and perceived interference in the functioning of the Central Bureau of Investigation (CBI).

2. The P. Chidambaram Case:

The P. Chidambaram case refers to a legal matter involving P. Chidambaram, a prominent figure in Indian politics.

P. Chidambaram, a prominent figure within the Indian National Congress, was confronted with allegations pertaining to acts of corruption and money laundering. The arrest that took place in August 2019 was widely perceived as having political motivations, with the timing of the arrest being interpreted as a deliberate strategy to shift public focus away from other matters.

3. The Investigation into Robert Vadra

Robert Vadra, the individual who is married to Sonia Gandhi's daughter and is associated with the Congress party, has been subjected to thorough investigations conducted by the Enforcement Directorate (ED) in relation to his purported engagement in contentious land transactions. Critics contend that the aforementioned investigations were driven by political motivations and strategically aimed at singling out a prominent figure within the opposition.

4. The West Bengal Standoff:

The West Bengal Standoff refers to a situation of conflict or confrontation that has occurred in the state of West Bengal.

The political discord between the Central Government and the West Bengal State Government, under the leadership of Mamata Banerjee, reached its pinnacle during the 2019 Lok Sabha elections. The Central Bureau of Investigation's endeavour to interrogate the Kolkata Police Commissioner resulted in a state of impasse, as Mamata Banerjee alleged that the Modi government was employing federal agencies as a means to intimidate political adversaries.

5. the Farmer Protests and the Disha Ravi Case.

Criticism was directed towards the Enforcement Directorate (ED) and Delhi Police for their alleged targeting of activists and journalists who expressed support for the farmers' cause during the farmer protests of 2020-2021. The apprehension of climate activist Disha Ravi on charges of sedition was perceived as an endeavour to stifle opposition.

4.7 Implications and Concerns

The present discourse aims to explore the implications and concerns associated with the subject matter at hand.

The purported misapplication of central agencies, such as the Central Bureau of Investigation (CBI) and the Enforcement Directorate (ED), carries substantial ramifications for the democratic fabric and legal framework of India. Several significant concerns and potential consequences arise from the situation at hand.

1. Erosion of Public Trust:

One significant issue that has emerged in recent years is the erosion of public trust. The erosion of public trust in central agencies and the undermining of their credibility occur when these institutions are perceived as being utilised for political vendettas. This phenomenon has the potential to undermine the integrity of the legal system and impede the attainment of equitable outcomes.

2. Chilling Effect on Dissent:

The apprehension of becoming a target of central agencies can potentially exert a deterrent influence on the expression of dissent and oppositional viewpoints, resulting in self-imposed restrictions on speech and a hesitancy to openly articulate political beliefs.

3. The erosion of democratic values.

The vitality of a robust democratic system is contingent upon the fundamental tenets of transparency, accountability, and the presence of checks and balances. The purported misapplication of central agencies has the potential to undermine these core democratic principles.

4. Damage to Federalism:

One significant consequence that arises from this situation is the potential harm inflicted upon the principle of federalism.

The utilisation of central agencies to specifically target state governments has the potential to undermine the fundamental tenets of federalism and the delineation of powers between the central and state governments.

5. The influence on foreign investments.

International investors may exhibit caution when considering investment opportunities in a nation where the integrity of the legal system is believed to be compromised. Accusations regarding the improper utilisation of entities such as the Enforcement Directorate (ED) have the potential to discourage foreign investments and adversely impact the Indian economy.

4. 8The Government's Perspective

In order to present a comprehensive and impartial analysis, it is imperative to take into account the viewpoint of the government regarding these allegations. The government posits that its actions are primarily aimed at preserving the integrity of the legal system and addressing issues related to corruption and financial misconduct. As per statements made by government officials, impartial investigations and raids are conducted, with an explicit denial of any political motivations underlying these measures.

Advocates aligned with the government assert the imperative of scrutinizing instances of corruption and economic transgressions, irrespective of the political affiliations of the implicated parties. The authors contend that these investigations are integral components of a wider endeavour to Enhance governance and eradicate corruption within the realm of public affairs.

4.9 Possible Reform Strategies

1. Strengthening Institutional Independence

One crucial aspect to consider in enhancing the effectiveness and credibility of institutions is the reinforcement of institutional independence.

The implementation of reforms aimed at safeguarding the autonomy of investigative agencies such as the Central Bureau of Investigation (CBI) and the Enforcement Directorate (ED) is of paramount importance. This encompasses measures such as safeguarding these agencies against political intervention, bolstering their independence, and implementing more transparent procedures for the appointment of their leaders.

2. Mechanisms for Oversight:

The implementation of effective oversight mechanisms, such as parliamentary committees and judicial review, can play a crucial role in ensuring that these agencies adhere to legal boundaries and uphold transparency in their activities.

3. Legal Reforms have been proposed as a means to address existing shortcomings and improve the effectiveness of the legal system.

Another potential avenue for reform involves the reevaluation and modification of pertinent legislation to mitigate the potential for misuse of agencies such as the Central Bureau of Investigation (CBI) and the Enforcement Directorate (ED). Enhancing the precision of delineating their jurisdiction and powers can effectively mitigate ambiguity and the risk of potential political intervention.

4. the concept of accountability measures.

It is imperative to implement mechanisms that ensure the accountability of officials in the event of any potential misuse of these agencies. The imposition of consequences on individuals who abuse their authority can serve as a deterrent.

5. the relationship between public awareness and media freedom.

Promoting public consciousness regarding the significance of maintaining the rule of law and safeguarding the autonomy of investigative agencies is of utmost importance. An independent and dynamic media that is able to report without apprehension is equally crucial in ensuring governmental and institutional transparency and responsibility.

The purported misuse of central agencies such as the Central Bureau of Investigation (CBI) and the Enforcement Directorate (ED) for political objectives has emerged as a highly debated topic within the realm of Indian politics. While the government asserts its dedication to preserving the principles of the rule of law and addressing issues of corruption, detractors contend that these governmental bodies are being utilised to selectively target political adversaries and suppress dissenting viewpoints. The controversies pertaining to the Central Bureau of Investigation (CBI) and the Enforcement Directorate (ED) carry substantial ramifications for the democratic fabric of India, the confidence of the public, and the integrity of the legal system.

The implementation of reforms aimed at bolstering the autonomy and clarity of these agencies, establishing strong mechanisms for oversight, and ensuring that officials are held responsible for any wrongdoing are imperative measures to effectively address these concerns. Ensuring a harmonious coexistence of law enforcement and upholding democratic values and the rule of law is of paramount importance for the trajectory of Indian political landscape. It is imperative for the Indian government and its officials, including Prime Minister Narendra Modi, to effectively acknowledge and redress these concerns in order to guarantee the impartial and accountable functioning of these agencies, devoid of any political intervention.

4.10 The Negative Impacts of Narendra Modi's Extended Tenure in Governance in India and the Significance of Leadership Transition

Narendra Modi, the incumbent Prime Minister of India, assumed office in May 2014 and subsequently secured a second term in May 2019 through re-election. Although he has garnered substantial popularity among a considerable segment of the Indian populace, there are growing apprehensions regarding the adverse consequences associated with his prolonged tenure in power. The objective of this essay is to examine the adverse ramifications of Modi's prolonged tenure and emphasise the significance of the transfer of power from one leader to another within a democratic system.

I. The Erosion of Democratic Values

The potential erosion of democratic values is considered to be one of the most significant negative consequences associated with an extended tenure in power. In the context of a dynamic democratic system such as India, it is imperative that leaders are subject to the principle of accountability to the citizenry, which is effectively achieved through periodic electoral processes. The prolonged tenure of a leader carries the potential for the consolidation of power and the gradual erosion of mechanisms that ensure accountability and balance. This phenomenon has the potential to give rise to authoritarian inclinations, wherein the leader and their political party exhibit diminished responsiveness towards the public's needs and demands.

The prolonged tenure of Narendra Modi has elicited apprehensions regarding the concentration of authority within the governing Bharatiya Janata Party (BJP) and his leadership. As power becomes increasingly centralised, the process of decision-making tends to become less transparent and lacks the necessary level of accountability towards the general public. The sustenance of a robust democracy hinges upon the periodic transfer of power, which serves to uphold a harmonious equilibrium among diverse institutions and guarantee the government's continued receptiveness to the populace's needs and apprehensions.

II. Diminishment of Resistance

One detrimental outcome associated with extended periods of leadership is the gradual erosion of opposition parties. In the context of a democratic system, the opposition assumes a crucial function by ensuring governmental accountability and presenting alternative policies and ideas. When a single political party maintains control over a prolonged duration, the ability of opposing parties to effectively engage in competition can be significantly hindered.

Under Prime Minister Narendra Modi's leadership, the Bharatiya Janata Party (BJP) has significantly strengthened its position in the Indian political landscape. This has been achieved through a series of victories in state elections, which have not only solidified the party's control but also resulted in a reduction of the clout held by regional and national opposition parties. The consolidation of power has the potential to result in a system dominated by a single political party, which is detrimental to the principles of democratic governance. The absence of a robust opposition can lead to diminished examination of governmental policies and actions, as well as a deterioration of political pluralism.

III. Decreased Accountability

Extended tenure in office can also lead to reduced levels of responsibility. When leaders are aware of their prolonged tenure, they may exhibit reduced responsiveness towards the immediate concerns of the public, potentially prioritising long-term political survival at the expense of the welfare of the citizens. The effectiveness of accountability mechanisms, such as elections and parliamentary oversight, diminishes when leaders maintain their positions of authority for prolonged durations.

Under the leadership of Prime Minister Modi, there have been occurrences that have raised concerns regarding accountability. Critics contend that the government's level of accountability regarding matters such as the management of the COVID-19 pandemic, the economic recession, and diverse social and political predicaments has been inadequate. Increasing the frequency of power transitions has the potential to augment the government's capacity to address these issues in a more timely and effective manner.

IV. The Phenomenon of Polarization and Divisiveness

The extended duration of leadership has the potential to foster polarisation and divisiveness within a nation. Longevity in leadership roles can lead to increased entrenchment and reduced inclination to engage in compromise or pursue consensus. This phenomenon has the potential to contribute to a heightened level of polarisation within the political sphere, wherein ideological disparities are emphasised, and the nature of political dialogue becomes progressively hostile.

Under Prime Minister Modi's leadership, India has experienced an increase in polarisation based on religious and ideological affiliations. Critics contend that the policies and rhetoric employed by the individual in question have played a role in fostering an environment characterised by heightened communal and sectarian tensions. Frequent changes in leadership have the potential to introduce fresh perspectives and potentially mitigate the intensity of divisions within an organisation.

V. Economic and Social Policies

The extended tenure in authority can yield consequences for both economic and social policies. Leaders who maintain their positions for an extended duration may exhibit a decreased propensity to embrace novel concepts and implement reforms. Economic policies, specifically, may experience stagnation as governments exhibit reduced inclination towards implementing substantial changes that could potentially incur short-term political costs.

Critics contend that the government led by Prime Minister Modi has been characterised by a sluggish pace of economic reforms, with inadequate emphasis on pressing concerns such as unemployment and economic disparity. Frequent changes in leadership have the potential to introduce new policy priorities and innovations aimed at addressing the dynamic demands of society.

VI. The Role of Media in Safeguarding Freedom of Expression

The media and freedom of expression play integral roles in the effective operation of a democratic system. The perpetuation of leadership over an extended period can lead to a media landscape that is less diverse and independent, as governments endeavour to exert control or manipulate the prevailing narrative. The potential ramifications of this phenomenon on the accessibility and reliability of information for the general public may be predominantly adverse.

Under the leadership of Prime Minister Modi, there have been apprehensions regarding the condition of media freedom and the autonomy of journalists. Critics contend that media organisations have encountered external pressures to engage in self-censorship or conform to the government's agenda. The implementation of new leadership has the potential to revitalise the media industry and safeguard the fundamental right of freedom of speech.

VII. The Erosion of Institutions

Extended periods of leadership can also result in the deterioration of institutions. As leaders engage in the process of consolidating power, it is possible for institutions that are intended to serve as mechanisms for checks and balances to experience a decline in their effectiveness or be influenced to align with the leader's objectives. This phenomenon has the potential to result in a decrease in the efficacy and autonomy of crucial establishments such as the judiciary, law enforcement agencies, and regulatory bodies.

Concerns have been raised by critics regarding the autonomy and ethical conduct of specific institutions throughout Prime Minister Modi's tenure. Frequent transitions in leadership can contribute to the restoration of institutional integrity and bolster their commitment to upholding the rule of law and safeguarding the rights of citizens.

4.11 The significance of leadership transitions

When examining the adverse consequences of extended leadership, it is crucial to underscore the importance of leadership transitions within a democratic framework. Frequent leadership changes provide numerous advantages that contribute to the effective operation of democratic systems:

1. Accountability: Leadership transitions afford periodic opportunities for the general public to exercise their right to hold their leaders accountable via electoral processes. This practise ensures that leaders maintain their ability to effectively address the evolving needs and concerns of the populace.

2. The Revitalization of Concepts: Frequent shifts in leadership facilitate the introduction of fresh perspectives and ideas into the realm of governance. This has the potential to result in the development of novel policies and reforms that effectively tackle emerging challenges.

3. The phenomenon of political pluralism is facilitated by leadership transitions, as they create avenues for multiple political parties and ideologies to engage in competition and effectively represent the wide range of perspectives held by the citizenry.

4. The maintenance of institutional health is facilitated by leadership changes, which play a crucial role in preserving the effectiveness of democratic institutions in upholding the rule of law and safeguarding the rights of citizens.

5. Mitigation of Polarization: Frequent changes in leadership have the potential to mitigate political polarization by presenting the opportunity for new leaders who prioritize consensus-building and the pursuit of compromise.

6. The process of leadership transitions can result in the implementation of new policies and a heightened emphasis on addressing prevailing economic and social issues, thereby fostering adaptability and responsiveness to changing conditions.

The extended tenure of Narendra Modi in power in India has elicited apprehensions regarding the adverse consequences associated with prolonged leadership, such as the erosion of democratic principles, the weakening of opposition, reduced accountability, heightened polarisation, and potential ramifications for economic and social policies. Regular leadership transitions play a vital role in preserving the robustness of democratic systems, fostering a sense of responsibility, and introducing novel concepts and viewpoints into the realm of governance. In the context of a dynamic democracy such as India, it becomes imperative to establish a harmonious equilibrium between the continuity of leadership and the necessity for leadership changes, in order to uphold the democratic principles that form the foundation of the country's political framework.

Chapter Five

Conclusion

In a global context characterised by the continuous evolution of power dynamics and governance structures over extended periods, the inquiry into the necessity of governmental change at specific intervals remains a topic of enduring importance. The examination of this significant matter, utilising the perspectives of prominent figures such as Vladimir Putin and Xi Jinping, alongside an analysis of power transitions in the historical context of the Roman Empire, has provided valuable insights into the intricate nature of this subject. The perspectives on power transfer from major world religions, including Christianity, Islam, Judaism, and Hinduism, have been thoroughly examined in our study. As the culmination of our expedition approaches, it is imperative to engage in introspection regarding the knowledge we have acquired and the wider ramifications for present-day civilization.

The instances of Vladimir Putin's tenure in Russia and Xi Jinping's leadership in China have exemplified the potential drawbacks associated with extended periods of governance. The long-lasting tenure of Putin, in spite of his indisputable achievements in the economic stabilisation of Russia and the restoration of its global standing, has concurrently elicited apprehensions regarding the regression of democratic principles, a dearth of political diversity, and violations of human rights. The consolidation of power by Xi Jinping in China has yielded remarkable economic growth and enhanced global recognition. However, this process has also been accompanied by heightened state control, the suppression of dissent, and a potential disregard for democratic principles.

When examining the historical context of the Roman Empire, it becomes evident that the matter of power transition is not a novel phenomenon. The Roman Empire underwent various transitions of power, encompassing hereditary succession as well as instances of military coups and assassinations. The frequent changes in leadership within the Empire resulted in a combination of advantageous and disadvantageous outcomes, ultimately playing a significant role in the ascent and decline of the Empire. The aforementioned historical viewpoint provides a significant lesson, underscoring the significance of adaptability and resilience within the realm of governance.

Moreover, our investigation into religious viewpoints regarding the transfer of power has highlighted the wide range of beliefs and values that influence our individual perspectives on the world. Christianity places significant emphasis on the virtues of humility, service, and the ultimate authority of a transcendent deity. The Islamic faith promotes the principles of consultation and consensus in matters of leadership while simultaneously highlighting the significance of justice and compassion. The teachings of Judaism advocate for principles of justice, righteousness, and the notion of a select community.

Hinduism, characterised by a multitude of deities and a wide range of philosophical perspectives, exemplifies the intricate and adaptable nature of its leadership principles.

It is evident that the inquiry regarding the necessity for governments to undergo changes over a specific period is a complex matter. The analysis of the leadership styles of Putin and Xi, the historical trajectory of the Roman Empire, and the perspectives derived from prominent global religions collectively indicate that a universally applicable solution cannot be readily identified. However, it is evident that the need for governance reform is contingent upon various elements, such as the particular circumstances, the actions undertaken by the leader, and the changing requirements and aspirations of the governed populace.

The examination of Vladimir Putin and Xi Jinping's cases demonstrates that leaders have the capacity to attain notable accomplishments throughout their time in office. However, it is important to acknowledge that this can also result in the accumulation of unbridled authority, thereby raising apprehensions regarding authoritarian tendencies, human rights violations, and limitations on political liberties. Effective mitigation of these challenges is contingent upon the implementation of comprehensive mechanisms for oversight and accountability within the political framework, an unwavering commitment to democratic tenets, and the preservation of fundamental human rights. The implementation of a leadership transition system can serve as a preventive measure against the concentration of power, which has the potential to result in abusive practices and the erosion of democratic principles.

The tenure of Narendra Modi as the leader of India has been characterised by a multifaceted combination of accomplishments and controversies. Although his period in office has been characterised by economic expansion and the advancement of infrastructure, it has also given rise to apprehensions regarding the deterioration of democratic principles, the escalation of societal disparities, and the marginalisation of minority perspectives. Concerns have arisen regarding the state of Indian democracy due to the consolidation of power within the ruling party and the erosion of checks and balances.

The transfer of power to a new leader is imperative in order to foster a more robust democratic system. A transition in leadership has the potential to introduce novel viewpoints, foster inclusiveness, and restore confidence in democratic establishments. Additionally, it can function as a safeguard against the potential development of authoritarian inclinations that may arise during prolonged periods in power. The regular and peaceful transfer of power is a fundamental tenet of democracy, serving to ensure accountability, uphold constitutional principles, and cultivate a diverse and dynamic society. For the preservation and enhancement of India's democratic system, a transition in leadership is imperative and advantageous.

Conversely, the historical account of the Roman Empire serves as a testament to the difficulties and repercussions associated with frequent shifts in leadership. While certain transitions exhibited competence and progress, others resulted in instability and even chaos. This historical analysis elucidates the importance of conscientiously evaluating the frequency of power transfer within the wider framework of a society's exigencies and obstacles. The possession of flexibility in leadership transitions, when deemed necessary, can prove to be a highly advantageous attribute.

Religious viewpoints regarding the transfer of power emphasise the importance of moral and ethical principles in the realm of governance. Christianity, due to its emphasis on the virtues of humility and service, serves as a reminder that individuals in positions of leadership ought to adopt a servant-like role towards the populace, guided by a moral authority of greater significance. The emphasis placed by Islam on consultation and justice highlights the significance of community engagement in the process of decision-making and the establishment of governance that is fair and equitable. The principles of justice and righteousness within Judaism advocate for the appointment of leaders who prioritise the welfare of the community and adhere to ethical norms. The diverse and intricate nature of Hinduism permits a broad spectrum of governance approaches, thereby exemplifying the imperative for leadership to be adaptable.

Upon careful examination of these perspectives, it becomes evident that the issue of transitioning governments after a specific period is not a fixed binary choice between "always" or "never." However, the issue at hand pertains to achieving equilibrium and flexibility. The determination of power transfer frequency should be predicated upon societal requirements and complexities, and it ought to be guided by principles that accord precedence to democratic values, human rights, and ethical leadership.

Furthermore, when contemplating the instances involving Putin and Xi, it is imperative to acknowledge the significance of robust institutions, an independent media, and an active civil society in upholding leaders' responsibility and safeguarding against the consolidation of power within a select few individuals. The historical insights derived from the Roman Empire serve as a poignant reminder that effective leadership necessitates adaptability and responsiveness to the evolving circumstances of their era. Furthermore, leaders ought to prioritise the establishment of enduring institutions that transcend their own tenure in order to foster long-lasting societal structures.

From a religious standpoint, it is apparent that the exercise of power should be accompanied by qualities such as humility, justice, and a dedication to the welfare of individuals. Leaders ought to be guided by moral and ethical principles, irrespective of their religious or philosophical orientations. The underlying theme present in each of these religious viewpoints is the notion that effective leadership ought to be motivated by a profound sense of accountability and a dedication to the collective welfare.

The inquiry regarding the necessity for governments to undergo changes over time is a complex and multifaceted matter. The correct response may vary depending on the specific context. It is evident, nonetheless, that the utilisation of leadership authority ought to be directed towards the advancement of the populace, and it should be enacted with a profound commitment to accountability, modesty, and ethical comportment. The significance of balance, adaptability, and the enduring values of democracy, human rights, and ethical leadership is underscored by the illustrations of Putin and Xi, the teachings derived from the Roman Empire, and the perspectives offered by major world religions.

In contemporary times, humanity has observed both favourable and unfavourable outcomes stemming from extended periods of leadership. The instance involving Vladimir Putin and Xi Jinping highlights the inherent risks associated with unrestrained authority and autocratic inclinations. Although both leaders have successfully fostered substantial economic growth and political stability throughout their respective tenures, their governance has also elicited apprehensions regarding the potential erosion of democratic values, instances of human rights violations, and a dearth of political diversity.

The tenure of President Putin in Russia, characterised by the implementation of constitutional amendments enabling the extension of his presidency, has garnered disapproval from both domestic and international analysts. The aforementioned action has elicited apprehensions regarding the consolidation of authority within the purview of an individual and the gradual deterioration of democratic establishments. In a parallel vein, the elimination of term limits by Xi Jinping in China has effectively consolidated his status as the preeminent leader, resulting in a heightened concentration of authority.

The experiences of Vladimir Putin and Xi Jinping illustrate the imperative for implementing mechanisms that foster accountability, transparency, and the peaceful transition of power. Within democratic systems, various mechanisms are incorporated to safeguard against the accumulation of power, including the implementation of periodic elections and term limits. These measures are specifically devised to mitigate the potential consolidation of authority. The aforementioned characteristics of democratic governance serve to establish a system wherein leaders are held responsible for the populace while also facilitating a smooth and organised transfer of authority.

The historical example of the Roman Empire offers additional understanding regarding the significance of effectively managed power transitions. The Roman Empire underwent a diverse array of leadership transitions, encompassing hereditary succession, military coups, and assassinations. Certain transitions were characterised by capable and efficient leadership, whereas others led to instability, turmoil, and even internal conflicts.

This historical account serves as a poignant reminder that the frequency at which power is transferred ought to be meticulously deliberated within the wider framework of a society's exigencies and obstacles. The occurrence of frequent leadership changes has the potential to generate instability within an organisation or system, whereas infrequent transitions may facilitate the concentration of power and create opportunities for its misuse.

The achievement of effective governance necessitates the establishment of a harmonious equilibrium that is capable of promptly adapting to the distinctive conditions prevailing over a particular period of time.

Shifting our focus towards the viewpoints of prominent global religions, it becomes evident that each respective tradition offers a distinct perspective through which the matter of power transfer can be examined. Christianity, as an illustrative example, places significant emphasis on the virtues of humility and service as fundamental qualities for individuals in positions of leadership. According to the teachings of Jesus, individuals in positions of leadership are tasked with assuming the role of servants to the populace, actively striving to address their requirements and uphold ethical principles. Christianity serves as a reminder of the paramount authority held by a divine power, which ought to serve as a guiding force for human leadership.

In contrast, Islam advocates for the principle of shura, which entails engaging in consultation as a means of making decisions. This principle advocates for leaders to actively solicit the viewpoints of the community and achieve a collective agreement regarding matters of governance. Moreover, Islam emphasises the significance of justice, compassion, and fairness in the realm of leadership. Leaders are tasked with the responsibility of upholding these principles, thereby ensuring that their authority is exercised with sagacity and ethical accountability.

Judaism, due to its emphasis on principles of justice and righteousness, promotes the prioritisation of the collective welfare of its leaders and advocates for their adherence to moral values. The concept of a select group of individuals entrusted with the duty of maintaining the covenant with a divine entity serves to emphasise the moral aspect of leadership. Within the context of Hinduism, the multifaceted and intricate religious tradition encompasses a broad spectrum of philosophical and practical perspectives pertaining to the domain of governance. The presence of multiple deities and diverse philosophical traditions within Hinduism exemplifies the necessity for leaders to possess adaptability and flexibility.

The inquiry regarding the necessity for governments to undergo change within a specific timeframe is a multifaceted and intricate matter. It is apparent that there is no universally applicable solution, and the need for governance reform is contingent upon a multitude of factors, encompassing the particular circumstances, the actions undertaken by the leader, and the evolving requirements and aspirations of the governed society. The analysis conducted on the leadership of Putin and Xi, the historical examination of the Roman Empire, and the insights derived from major world religions collectively indicate that the frequency of power transfer ought to be governed by principles that place democratic values, human rights, and ethical leadership at the forefront.

In order to achieve optimal equilibrium, it is of utmost importance that we derive valuable insights from the leadership experiences of individuals such as Putin and Xi. This will enable us to maintain a system where authority is held responsible and democratic structures are preserved. The historical lessons derived from the Roman Empire serve as a poignant reminder of the significance of adaptability and resilience in the realm of governance. These qualities enable leaders to effectively address the evolving circumstances of their era.

Furthermore, religious viewpoints regarding the transfer of power impart to us the lasting significance of moral and ethical principles in the realm of leadership. Irrespective of an individual's religious or philosophical beliefs, a recurring theme in these teachings is the notion that leaders ought to be driven by a sense of accountability and a dedication to the collective welfare. The guiding principles for individuals in positions of authority should encompass humility, justice, compassion, and ethical conduct.

In the contemporary global landscape, characterised by diverse political systems and societal norms, it is imperative to adopt an open-minded perspective and uphold democratic principles when considering the matter of governmental transformation. The significance of achieving an optimal equilibrium between stability and change in governance is underscored by the knowledge gained from the experiences of Putin and Xi, the historical lessons derived from the Roman Empire, and the wisdom imparted by major world religions.

In order to ascertain the extent of government change following a specific period, it is imperative to possess a comprehensive comprehension of the distinctive circumstances and obstacles encountered by each society. The foundation of this should be firmly grounded in a steadfast dedication to the fundamental tenets of democracy, human rights, and the practice of ethical leadership. In progressing further, it is imperative that we endeavour to establish political systems that cultivate accountability, transparency, and the nonviolent transfer of authority, all while upholding the fundamental principles that are crucial for the welfare of society as a whole.

References

www.ingramcontent.com/pod-product-compliance
Lightning Source LLC
LaVergne TN
LVHW061541070526
838199LV00077B/6862